THE SUPREME
ADVENTURE

THE SUPREME
ADVENTURE

The Experience of
Siddha Yoga

PETER HAYES

Delta

Published by
Dell Publishing
a division of
The Bantam Doubleday Dell Publishing Group, Inc.
666 Fifth Avenue
New York, New York 10103

Printed in the United States of America

Library of Congress Cataloging in Publication Data
Hayes, Peter, 1948–
   The supreme adventure.
   Bibliography: p.
   1. Yoga, Siddha.   I. Title.
BL1238.56.S53H39   1988   294.5′4   87-36410
ISBN 0-440-55002-5
September 1988

10 9 8 7 6 5 4 3 2 1

BG

To my Mother —
in her many forms

Table of Contents

Foreword

Most of us live with a sense of unfulfilled promise, with goals that elude our striving, with an intuition of our own possibilities that all our efforts at work and love can satisfy only partially. Some of us come closer than others to fulfillment, yet few of us, if we are honest, would say that we have become everything we want to be.

This is a book about the path of true becoming, where our promise is realized and our dreams come true. It is a book, as the author tells us on the first page, about the supreme adventure, the ultimate quest, that journey from which we return transformed.

The spiritual path has existed since the beginning of human history. Yet, though we know it exists, most of us regard it as the prerogative of rare, special people: born mystics, or saints capable of intense and difficult austerities. It never occurs to most of us that the inner journey is accessible to us, and not only accessible but imperative. The goals we wish for, the qualities we admire and long to develop, the contentment we desire, can only be satisfied by a serious inner quest, as anyone can testify who has tapped the infinite resources of energy and strength that lie within the human heart. The problem is that for most of us the inner country is obscure, like any other unfamiliar territory, and that the maps which have been made of it vary immensely. Although for ages people have been taking this path and leaving records of their journey, some of their maps are reliable, and some are wildly misleading. Some lead through muddy country and quicksand; others through straight roads over high ground.

This is the great value of Peter Hayes's book. What he has given us is a clear and straightforward account of one of the most ancient and powerful roads to self-fulfillment. Writing with humor as well as with a laserlike ability to cut through mystical obscurantism, Hayes has put together a handbook of the inner secrets, examining the whys and hows of the interior life in an extraordinarily clear, practical, and immediate fashion.

What Hayes is sharing with us is his own inner journey. Before he began on it, he was a New York writer in his early thirties, a person used to burying his longings in jobs well done or games well played, a person whose interest in spiritual questions was mostly academic. Then he came into contact with Swami Muktananda, the great Indian saint who awakened the dormant spiritual energy in so many people. Hayes's awakening was a particularly dramatic one, and he soon found himself exploring inner worlds he had not known existed, and uncovering qualities in himself he had never imagined were there. The secret behind this inner unfoldment, he discovered, was *Shaktipat,* a transmission of grace and spiritual power from Master to disciple. And with this transmission began his relationship first with Baba Muktananda, and later with Baba's spiritual successor, Gurumayi Chidvilasananda. It is this relationship, Hayes tells us, that is the real key to the extraordinary inner growth process he describes. By following the age-old teachings and day-to-day guidance of these two great saints, Hayes opened himself to the continuing transmission of their spiritual power, an ongoing infusion of energy which allowed him to experience states of inner awareness that he could never have achieved on his own.

This relationship has meant learning how to rely on the instructions of the Master as well as on the subtle guidance of the awakened power within him. And as this book makes clear, it has given him an ability to see himself and his world in an entirely fresh way, experiencing a wholeness and clarity of being which are not so much learned as imbibed from the Master.

What Hayes conveys to us, however, is not just his own personal story, for his book is not an autobiography but the record of a discovery which, as he points out, is available to anyone who truly wants it. He takes us step-by-step along the path, describing the initial awakening and the experiences that followed. He also explains the stages of meditation and the dynamics of the Master–disciple relationship.

Some of the most moving passages in the book are those which evoke the quality of life around Gurumayi Chidvilasananda, in whose presence Hayes experienced a palpable current of freedom and love. It is this freedom, this love, which are the goal of the spiritual journey. With great simplicity and power, Peter Hayes shows us what it is like to glimpse this perfect love, and what happens to us when we follow the road to its fulfillment.

—Swami Durgananda
(formerly Sally Kempton)
South Fallsburg, New York
September 17, 1987

Preface

Siddha Yoga is the eternal path.

Just as when a tree bears fruit, the fruit is not different from the tree, so Siddha Yoga is both the means to the attainment and the attainment itself. It is both the journey and its destination.

Siddha means "perfected," yoga means "to unite." Siddha Yoga is perfection in unity.

An ancient path, it exists of itself. Neither the branch of any sect nor the tendril of any religion, it is its own perfect support. By treading this path, countless seekers have realized their own Self and have imparted its wisdom to others who have yearned to know life's purpose and to experience the Supreme Reality.

Anyone can follow this path, but no one need follow it blindly. In Siddha Yoga, the seeker receives the grace and guidance of one who has become enlightened while traveling on the same path. Such a being is called a Guru.

The Guru purges the seeker of worldly ignorance and bestows upon him a direct experience of the light of the Supreme Reality. Through Shaktipat, the Guru transmits his own fully awakened energy into the seeker, and the seeker's own inner energy, the kundalini, *is awakened in turn. Thus, the process of Siddha Yoga begins to unfold.*

Upon the awakening of his kundalini by Guru's grace,

the seeker spontaneously experiences his own divinity. Before, he had been shrouded in his limited awareness of himself and had led his life accordingly. But now, his divine awareness having been kindled by the Guru, he no longer regards himself as isolated and limited but as one with the Supreme Reality, the source of all life in the cosmos.

Through Siddha Yoga, perfection in unity, the seeker is certain to experience his relationship with the God who dwells within. Jesus said, "God's kingdom is within you." Swami Muktananda, who propagated Siddha Yoga in our time, said, "God dwells within you as you." Over the centuries the saints have spread this truth: What you are searching for lies within you.

Through Guru's grace alone can the ultimate wisdom be obtained. Nonetheless, Siddha Yoga offers techniques that aid the seeker in turning within. These include contemplation, mantra repetition, and meditation. To complement these practices, the seeker is encouraged to perform selfless service, to keep the company of others who are devoted to the Truth, to read books rich in divine wisdom, and to cultivate moderation by conserving his physical and mental energies.

Siddha Yoga is the yoga of grace. To receive grace, no preparation is required. Everyone speaks about worthiness, but the true meaning of worthiness is to welcome the grace that has already embraced you.

The scriptures say that through one word, one look, one touch, or through his will, the Guru can awaken a seeker's inner energy, giving him a direct experience of his inner Self. Many feel that they do not need a Guru or a spiritual path, that they can enlighten themselves on their own. But think how difficult it would be to become a gourmet chef without seeking any help—without even taking the support of pots or of food! Such a chef would stand on his own, in one spot, for a very long time; he could not even begin to prepare a meal.

A Guru who has already traveled a path, who has reached his own goal, can eliminate the pride that blocks a seeker from experiencing his divinity.

When you are in love, everything looks beautiful and appealing, yet this experience is transitory, limited. In the same way, when your divine energy is awakened, everything looks beautiful. The world becomes easy to accept. But this experience is everlasting.

Siddha Yoga teaches that your body is a temple and your soul the flame within it. Therefore, although you follow Siddha Yoga through Guru's grace, you are really following your own Self. You come to recognize that there is no difference between the outer Guru and the Guru you experience within. Because the Guru is not merely the physical body but the embodiment of divine energy, the experience of the Guru in your own soul reveals extraordinary phenomena in both your spiritual and worldly life, and finally unifies both realms. What wonders spring from the Guru! What amazing grace!

You remain as a disciple with the enlightened Guru until the Guru tells you, "You have attained everything. Now I command you to become the Guru." From then on, it is your responsibility to fulfill the command of the Guru and to live your life in accordance with it.

My Guru, Swami Muktananda, who revealed Siddha Yoga to the whole world in this century, gives a very simple and direct message:

> Meditate on your Self. Honor your Self.
> Respect your Self. Kneel to your Self.
> Your God dwells within you as you, for you.

*So for the sake of Supreme Love, practice and follow
this message. Whatever you do, do it with love, for Siddha Yoga is also the yoga of divine love.*

      —Gurumayi Chidvilasananda
      Ganeshpuri, India
      January 27, 1987

Acknowledgments

In addition to the many individuals whose insights and stories appear in these pages, the author wishes to thank the following people for their editorial assistance: Ellen Berliner, Cynthia Briggs, Barbara Hamilton, Hemananda, Swami Shantananda, Lise Vail, and, most especially, Patti Walker.

P.H.

Invocation

The world is the play of my mad Mother Chiti.
It is Her dance, Her song, Her dream, Her vision.
I don't understand people who say it conceals Her.

Does the cry of an infant conceal its existence?
Do the deeds of a hero decrease his fame?
Does a woman's beauty make her go unnoticed?
Does an author's work obscure his name?

In the same way, the world reveals God;
It does not conceal Her.
How could it be other?
It is She who has become
Both health and sickness,
Loss and riches,
Pleasure, pain.
She takes the form of men and mountains,
Nations, rivers, women, rain.

She is the seer, and all objects of perception,
And when nothing is seen, She is ignorance, too.
She is that road you will never walk down,
The hills of a land you will not see.
The broken mirror
Which will never hold your face again.

She is all there never was and is,
High and low,
Bad and good.

(She is your delinquent son,
Your broken heart, Senor,
Your rented room.)

Images in a mirror are not different from the mirror.
A dreamer is not different
From the figments of his dream.
So this world is not different from its Mother.
It is Her dance, Her song, Her dream, Her vision;
Her terrible vision full of fire and bliss!

Namdev says,
My Gurumayi showed me this:
Nothing but a picture of God
Looks like what it is!

THE SIDDHA PATH:
An Introduction

A hero sets off upon a great adventure. He meets a wise man who furnishes him with magic words or weapons. Thus armed, he travels to a fairy kingdom, an enchanted castle, or a far-off realm, seeking to reclaim a kidnaped maiden, a priceless treasure, or a Holy Grail. On his quest he encounters wonders beyond description, as well as monsters of a thousand kinds; but, armed with a pure heart and the wise man's power, he slays the dragon, liberates the treasure, and returns home with his prize.

This is humanity's favorite story. As a writer, I was amazed to find it the plot of tales and myths from every age and culture. Sometimes the hero's name is Lancelot, sometimes Luke Skywalker. In other tales he is known as Jesus, Krishna, Moses, Sinbad, or Gilgamesh. It is the basic plot of the *Iliad* and the *Odyssey,* Dante's *Divine Comedy,* the *Ramayana,* "Jack and the Beanstalk," *Raiders of the Lost Ark,* and the game "Dungeons and Dragons." The appeal and special excellence of this fable is that it can be appreciated on many levels—as a simple adventure story, or as the description of a spiritual journey.

Read in this light, the far-off kingdom, the Land Beneath the Waves, is the deepest part of our own being, that undiscovered country in whose inner depths primordial powers and magic jewels lie in wait to madden the unwary and enrich the brave. For while this journey is dangerous, its reward is great. In some tales it is the secret of immortality, in others the pearl of great price. Whoever can descend into this enchanted kingdom, seize the treasure, and return with it to the upper world is a hero or heroine indeed!

For years I dreamed of such an adventure, but as time went on I put away this childish dream. Buried treasure and enchanted kingdoms are the stuff of fairy tales, while the heroes who conquer them do not exist in the real world.

Still, like many quietly desperate people, I had the feeling there was more to life than I was experiencing, that there was a treasure lost inside me, a great potential aching to be released, which somehow, sadly, I could not seem to tap. Tolstoy tells of a crippled beggar who lived upon a little patch of ground. He was so poor that when he died, the townspeople buried him on the spot. No sooner had they started to dig his grave than they unearthed a rich cache of gold coins just below the surface. The poor man had been literally sitting upon a fortune, but had never known it.

I was not like this unfortunate person. I *knew* there was a treasure hidden inside me; I just didn't know how to get to it.

Then, in November 1979, I met the great Siddha Guru Swami Muktananda. In his keynote address that month in Boston to the International Transpersonal Psychology Conference, Muktananda confirmed the existence of that treasure I had known about, but as yet had not been able to find. He said:

> *You are not just what you think you are; you are more sublime, you are greater. Great and divine light*

exists inside you. Inside, there is a vast world which is worth seeing. It's a sublime world. Compared to a vision of that world, the external world is nothing. On the inside, you'll hear such beautiful music, divine sound. You'll experience so much bliss, so much joy, a divine flame. The deeper you go inside yourself, the more of this world you'll see. And once you find this joy inside, you'll experience that same joy in the outside world as well. Therefore, learn how to turn inside. To turn inside is meditation. Meditation is not merely a spiritual technique. It is the practice of joy. It makes your life really joyful. It makes all your actions very clean. When this happens, in this very world, we can live happily. This is not a religion. This is not a political party. To turn within and perceive your own Self does not go against any religion. Therefore, meditate on your own Self. Worship your own Self. Kneel to your own inner Self. Understand your own Self. Your God dwells within you—as you.

I am not exaggerating when I say that Muktananda's words were like a bolt of lightning that electrified my understanding and removed my pain. Instantly, something was unstopped inside me, and a tremendous joy arose in my heart. This happiness, I saw now, had always been there. Muktananda had not put it in me, he had only removed a little dirt and there the treasure was.

But what was even more exciting, I recognized in Swami Muktananda—a seventy-one-year-old Indian monk—the hero I had always wanted to become. Here was a man who had dedicated his life to the inner journey and, after thirty-five years of the most arduous spiritual practices, had returned home with the prize. The result of this victory was plain to see. Muktananda did not have a halo, exactly, but I understood for the first time why saints are depicted in this way. He radiated an indescribable power. In his presence I felt clear and whole and still. Here was a being who was master of his inner kingdom, a spiritual warrior who had fought his inner enemies and prevailed. The result? To say he was happy would be an understatement. He gave new meaning to the word.

One night in Santa Monica while he was speaking, there was a thunderclap directly overhead. The clap was stupendous, and everyone instinctively dove for the ground. Everyone but Muktananda. He did not even flinch. Afterward, he merely remarked upon the sound's great power. And I realized then, such equanimity could not be faked; his joy was unshakable. Nothing could disturb it. He had reached some place inside himself where pain and fear did not approach. He had found the pearl of great price, he had found the joy of his own inner Self. Describing it, he said: "This contentment is complete and beyond the senses. It does not depend on anything outside. This contentment is everlasting, indestructible. It does not decrease."

But even more fortunate, having completed his journey and attained this space of supreme joy, Muktananda was offering to serve as a guide for anyone wishing to make the journey for themselves. He warned that while this quest could be hazardous if attempted on one's own, it could be completed safely and readily with the help of a being who had reached the goal and knew the way.

In yoga, such a one is called a Siddha Guru—a Self-realized Teacher. Muktananda himself had been guided to the goal by his own master, the great Siddha Guru Bhagawan Nityananda.

This path of the Guru is immemorially old, coming down to us in the present day through a lineage of Siddha masters. Because a seeker completes his journey through the grace and guidance of a Siddha, an enlightened being, this path is known as Siddha Yoga.

The Upanishads, a collection of some of the world's oldest and most revered spiritual texts, say of it: "The supreme state, which may be attained on some paths after extreme hardship, can be attained without great difficulty on the Siddha path."[1] What's more, because the goal to which this path leads is inside us, in order to follow it there is no need to retire from the world, or to give up one's family life or occupation. As Muktananda's own Guru told him, "Your heart is the hub of all sacred places. Go there and roam."

And so, putting my trust in Muktananda, I started on the Siddha path. And, most unexpectedly, the moment I turned my attention within, my outer life dramatically changed. Though I had smoked tobacco for thirteen years, my addiction disappeared literally overnight. My health, my disposition, my relationships, even my writing, improved; meanwhile in meditation, I began to have glimpses of that inner country, of inner lights and inner sounds. With such experiences I began to feel I was not who I had thought I was. I was greater. I was more sublime. Nor was this merely the result of an intoxicated ego, for I began to feel that the universe itself, as well as other people, were just as great and beautiful, too.

Then, in October 1982, Swami Muktananda died. Before leaving this world, however, he brought a young monk to the culmination of her own inner journey, making her a Siddha Guru and passing on to her the full power and authority of the age-old Siddha lineage. Since then, this great one, Swami Chidvilasananda, has been my teacher and my guide.

With such a great being alive and teaching, the question arises, Who needs a book by me? Why light a lamp when the sun is shining? The answer is simply, The sun bids the lamp to light.

THE SHAPE OF THINGS TO COME

This book is a sketch of the inner country and of the Siddha path that leads to its heart. It is meant to be a glimpse and an invitation only, not a substitute for the adventure itself. Since I haven't reached the end of this journey, I must rely on the testimony of those who have: the masters of the Siddha tradition, particularly Swami Muktananda and Swami Chidvilasananda, whom I refer to respectfully in these pages as *Baba,* Father, and *Gurumayi,* an honorific title which means "filled with the Guru." Occasionally I have called upon the saints of other traditions to verify certain inner landmarks in order to emphasize the nonsectarian nature of this realm—for the inner world, like the outer one, belongs to all.

The first part of this book investigates the teachings of Siddha Yoga, while the second part explores the practices, including instructions on how to meditate.

Occasionally I employ a Sanskrit term. My purpose in using these words is not to mystify, but to make things more clear. As with any discipline, there are certain terms to master. For instance, if I were writing about medicine, I could refer to "that instrument you look through to see germs"—or I could call it a microscope. But there's another reason, as well. Just as the language of the Eskimos is said to contain a hundred words for "snow," Sanskrit is the language of yoga and meditation, and words like yoga, mantra, Siddha, and Guru have no exact equivalent in other tongues. Whenever I use such a word, however, I define it in the text, or in the glossary at the end.

This book, then, is the story of an adventure. You and I, dear Reader, are its heroine or hero. The treasure we must uncover is our own inner Self. The country where it dwells is in the depths of our being. Meditation is our magic carpet; the Siddha Guru our wise and faithful guide; the word that will protect us, the mantra *Om Namah Shivaya.*

To embark upon this journey is the supreme adventure. Placed before the marvels of this inner kingdom, all outer wonders pale.

Part I

THE VISION OF YOGA

In New Orleans, during Gurumayi Chidvilasa- nanda's first American tour, someone asked me, "How did you become interested in Eastern philoso- phy?"

The answer that came out of my mouth surprised even me. I said: "I don't give a damn about Eastern philosophy. All I ever wanted was to be happy. I'd try a philosophy that comes from the *moon* if it could give me that."

My response, while extreme, is not so unusual. In the West, many people flee at the mere mention of the word "philosophy." And with good cause. A lot of philosophy is dry and pedantic, with little relation to our experience or lives. When we think of a philosopher, we see a Greek in a toga—or a bearded European gentleman with a pipe and a furrowed brow, seated in an armchair, much too late at night, thinking.

But in parts of the East, philosophy means something different. The philosophy of yoga is called a *darshana,* which means, literally, "a vision," something *seen.* It has little to do with thinking. It's not a system we make up with our brain, but a discovery, an inner experience. Kabir (1440–1518), a great saint and poet of the Siddha tradition, says:

What Kabir talks about is only what he has
 lived through;
If you have not lived through something,
 it is not true.[1]

THE INNER WORLD

The exponents of yoga were not armchair philosophers but active and practical people. They knew that even the truest philosophy is worthless if we don't apply it to our lives. Nor were they interested in promoting some favorite theology. Reading the works of such masters as Patanjali (about 200 B.C.), the sages of Kashmir (about 1000 A.D.), or Swami Muktananda (1908–1982), one is struck by their modern—or more precisely, timeless—point of view. Their outlook is scientific, not "religious." Their words are not a catechism of what they *believe*, but a report of what they've *seen* and *heard*, like the log of an expedition. The only difference is that these spiritual explorers traveled within: their laboratory was the human body; their microscope, meditation; their object of study, their own inner Self.

What they discovered in the course of their inner journeys were universal, human truths. To call their discoveries "Eastern" is like calling the law of gravity "Western." The laws of physics are universal and are just as true today in Tokyo and Bombay as they were in Newton's England. Similarly, those metaphysical insights and principles discovered by the Indian sages are as applicable to life in twentieth-century America or Australia as they were on the banks of the Indus River five millennia ago.

Furthermore, these yogic scientists do not ask us to accept their claims on blind faith. The truth of their visions, they confidently assert, can be verified by anyone who embarks upon the inner journey.

Compare the similarity of the following reports composed by sages from different traditions over a period of three thousand years.

"As large as the universe outside, even so large is the universe within the lotus of the heart. Within it are heaven and earth, the sun, the moon, the lightning, and all the stars. . . . In [that world] there is a lake whose waters are like nectar and whosoever tastes thereof is straightway drunk with joy, while beside that lake is a tree which yields the juice of immortality."[2] So declare the Vedantic Upanishads around 500 B.C.

Two thousand years later, the poet-saint Kabir proclaims: "Why wander in the outer garden? In your body there is a garden, an endless world. . . . There the lamps of a million suns and moons are shining. . . . There joy arises as you drink the sweet honey that steeps the lotus of the heart. . . . There the sky is filled with music made without strings or fingers."[3]

While five hundred years after Kabir, Baba Muktananda says, "Go to that land where divine melodies resound, where truly delicious nectar flows, where the cool and tender light shines, where there blazes the brilliant light of a million suns. . . ."[4]

This is not philosophy but human experience. It is an invitation to Self-discovery. Nor can it be said to belong to any sect or religion, past or present, East or West.

For this reason, instead of "The Philosophy of Yoga," I've called this first part the darshana, or *"Vision* of Yoga."

YOGA

Kipling said, "East is East and West is West and never the twain shall meet," but, in fact, the cultures of India, Europe, and the Middle East spring from a single root, and continue to show evidence of their common origin. The word yoga is an excellent example of this. A Sanskrit word meaning "union," it derives from the same Indo-European root as the English yoke, for yoga's aim is to "yoke" or unite us with the source of our being, which it calls the Self.

Swami Muktananda traces yoga back to "time immemorial." "Siddha Yoga is the same as it was thousands of years ago. . . . Then there were yogis and sages who had transcended their minds, and Siddha Yoga was born from their arduous practices and ultimate perfection. Siddha Yoga is the teaching of those great beings who had fully attained the Truth and become one with Shiva, the supreme Guru and all-pervasive divine Consciousness."[5]

Modern archaeology, for its part, tends to confirm Muktananda's claim of the path's great antiquity. Seals found at Mohenjodaro carved with images of meditating yogis and of Shiva, the traditional Lord of Yoga, have been radiocarbon-dated to 2500 B.C. Probably the oldest certain evidence of yoga is a body found in Yugoslavia buried in the lotus posture, dating back to 6000 B.C.! In India, in 1982, Swami Muktananda was buried in an identical manner. This marks a continuum of at least eight thousand years—"time immemorial"—and makes yoga, without question, the oldest living spiritual tradition in the world.[6]

THE EIGHT CLASSICAL YOGAS

Yoga may be defined, then, as union with the Self—as well as the practices that lead to this union. Classically, there are eight forms of yoga. *Hatha yoga,* the form best-known in the West, attempts to unite us with our inner Self by stilling our mind and purifying our body through postures and physical movements. *Jnana yoga* seeks to effect this union through study and contemplation, while *raja yoga* concentrates on virtuous actions and austerities, along with meditation. *Bhakti yoga* is the path of love and devotion, while in *mantra yoga,* sound is used to achieve this union through the chanting of sacred words and scriptures and through repetition of the names of God. *Karma yoga* seeks union with the Self through selfless service. In *kundalini yoga* and *laya yoga,* the inner spiritual power is awakened and led upward through the various *chakras,* or subtle spiritual centers.

In all these yogas the seeker relies upon his own knowledge, skills, and willpower to achieve success—which is by no means assured. For example, certain hatha yoga postures can be harmful if improperly performed, while the inner power may be dangerous if awakened but unguided. Because of this, the scriptures say the path of yoga is sharper than a razor's edge. A Hindi poet compares it to "chewing peanuts made of steel."

SIDDHA YOGA

There is another yoga, however, that does not depend upon a seeker's limited skills or mental powers. On this path, a Siddha, or master yogi, activates a disciple's latent spiritual energy through a transmission of his or her own spiritual force. Once this inner awakening occurs, the eight classical yogas arise spontaneously as needed from within, leading the seeker step-by-step to a state of spiritual perfection.

This yoga is filled with fascinating wonders.[7] The newly initiated seeker may find himself spontaneously assuming yogic postures or falling effortlessly into deep states of meditation. He may feel himself filled with divine love or with a sudden understanding of spiritual truths. He may utter mantras he has never heard before, be inspired to compose works of spiritual literature or to serve humanity.

Because it incorporates the eight classical yogas, this path is sometimes called the *mahayoga,* or great yoga. Certain scriptures call it *devayana pantha,* "the way of the gods." This great yoga, which is at the root of all other yogas, is also known by the name of Siddha Yoga because it takes place through the grace of a Siddha Guru. When a seeker surrenders himself to such a Guru, the Guru makes certain that the disciple attains the goal.

THE PHILOSOPHIES BEHIND SIDDHA YOGA

Siddha Yoga is not a philosophy as such, but rather an age-old path to Self-realization. However, because this path is so ancient, universal, and profound, a number of great philosophical systems have arisen over the centuries to explain and describe it. Vedanta, Sankhya, and Kashmir Shaivism are three of the very highest.

These three great darshanas do not conflict, although each is unique. Rather, like different maps of the same country—one showing roads; the second, political divisions; the third, elevations—they complement each other, emphasizing different aspects of the same inner realm.

In the following section we'll be referring at times to

these three particular "maps" to help orient us on our inner journey. Bear in mind, however, that this journey to the Self is unique for every person and, furthermore, that the road map is not the road.

CHAPTER 1

THE SELF

To many it is not given to hear of the Self.
Many, though they hear of it, do not understand it.
Wonderful is he who speaks of it.
Intelligent is he who learns of it.
Blessed is he who, taught by a great Guru,
is able to understand it.

—Katha Upanishad

Human beings have a core of nectar; but living on the surface, we wander like outcasts, searching for a sweetness, peace, and joy we can never find. If we're fortunate, we may experience this sweetness for an hour or two, or glimpse, for an instant, the shadow of bliss. But these experiences never last for long. And when they end they only leave us hungrier and craving.

Despite this, we search for happiness in everything we do. From the time we get up in the morning to the hour we go to bed, what we eat and wear, the kind of car we drive, where we work and whom we marry—every decision in our life is made with an eye to our greater happiness and pleasure.

Why are human beings like this? Why are we so obsessed with finding joy?

According to the yogic scriptures, it is because happiness is our very nature. It's not something we can forget about for a year, a day, or even for a moment. It's who and what we really are.

THE GOOSE AND THE SCORPION

Swami Muktananda explained what was meant by "our nature" like this: A scorpion wanted to cross the Ganges River, so he called to a goose who was swimming happily in its midst. "O Goose," he said, "give me a ride on your back to the other side."

The goose looked at the scorpion and said, "Are you mad? You're a scorpion. I'm a goose. If I come anywhere near you, you'll sting me."

But the scorpion replied, "O Goose, I would never do a thing like that. For if I stung you while I was riding on your back, you'd die and I'd drown."

This appeal to reason persuaded the goose. He floated over to the bank. "All right," he said to the scorpion, "climb on."

So the scorpion climbed upon the goose's back and they started off. They'd only gone a little way, however, when the goose felt a terrible pain. He looked back over his shoulder at the scorpion in disbelief. "My God! You stung me!" he cried. "Why?"

And as the goose and the scorpion both sank beneath the waves, the scorpion said, "O Goose, I'm sorry. I couldn't help it. It's my *nature!*"

BLISS

According to yoga, bliss is our nature. This is why we can't help but look for it in everything we do. And because it is our nature, it's *always* there inside us, waiting to be felt.

To most of us this is a revolutionary concept. You mean, we ask, happiness doesn't come from the people, events, and things in my life?

No; according to yoga, joy comes from within. Certain situations merely serve as an occasion for that joy. We then confuse the joy with the experience that triggered it.

A mother once told me of an extraordinary morning she shared with her young son. She was washing clothes, the dryer was overloaded, and she had to sit on top of the machine to keep it from banging and crawling across the floor. Curious, her little boy climbed up to join her, and then . . . something magical happened, and they passed one of those sweet, sweet hours that sometimes transpire between a mother and child. She said she'd never felt their love so deeply. The child evidently felt it, too, for one morning a week later, when asked by his mother what he would like to do, he said, "Let's go sit on top of the dryer."

A five-year-old may be excused for thinking this way. And yet most of us are guilty of the same confusion. We visit a peaceful place and believe the serenity we feel is coming from the scenery, from the mountains and the still spring night. We think the delicious sense of security we feel comes from the lock on our door, our warm bed, or money in the bank. We meet another person and think the love we feel is coming from him or her, or from the enchanting words our beloved whispers in our ear— never stopping to consider that the love, security, or peace are always there inside us, just waiting to be felt.

Inside of us, the Siddhas say, there is an infinite reservoir of joy that is the source of all our worldly happiness and pleasure. When triggered by something in the outer world, a tiny trickle of this joy flows out into our experience of a sense-object and we taste it. We think the joy is in the object or event itself, but in fact we are tasting our own inner bliss. All the sweetness and love we experience in life flows from this secret heart, this sea of power. Everyone has this place inside them, but some are better at mining its riches than others. Uniting with this inner place is known as yoga. Yoga calls this place the inner Self.

But if that's the case, where exactly inside us is this Self and how do we attain it? This, of course, is the burning question.

THE FOUR STATES

According to the science of yoga, we have four bodies, not one. Depending upon what body we are in, we experience a different state of consciousness and a corresponding world. When we are in our first, or outermost, body, the physical one, we experience the waking state and the physical world.

But when we turn inward and go to sleep, we leave the waking state behind and enter into another body in a deeper part of our being. This second body, called the *subtle* body, corresponds to the dream state, and here we experience a purely mental world quite different from the physical one. Just as our physical body contains our brain and physical sense organs, this subtle body holds our mind, our inner senses, thoughts, and feelings.

If we descend deeper still, we reach a third body, which is beyond even our mind. This is called the *causal* body. We enter it in the state of dreamless sleep. Because this body is beyond the mind, we experience in it neither pain nor pleasure. Its world is a void. After several hours in this body, we return to the waking state refreshed, our fatigue removed, our appetite for life renewed. Why is that?

Because, yoga says, there is a fourth state, the state of the Self, which lies just beyond this state of dreamless sleep. The rest and refreshment we derive from sleep come from the fact that in deep sleep we go very close to this Self and draw from it a tiny fraction of its vitality and power. However, because in dreamless sleep we are in a state beyond our mind, we don't consciously experience this Self or remember it upon awaking. An Upanishad puts it this way: "Just as those ignorant of the spot might pass, time and time again, over a buried treasure and see it not, so do all creatures go nightly to that divine world in sleep and find it not."[1]

But suppose we knew about this treasure? Suppose one night when we went to sleep we kept on going, even deeper than sleep, and plunged with open eyes into our own nectarean core, so that its sweetness gushed inside of us like the liquid heart of a chocolate-covered cherry? What if, upon feeling the least trickle of joy, we followed it inward to its source? Wouldn't we discover an ocean of happiness?

This turning of our attention inward toward the source of our joy is the principle behind yoga and meditation.

THE PERFECT "I"

The Self is the source of more than our joy, however. According to yoga, it's the source of our true identity as well. The Self is who we really are. It's for this reason Baba Muktananda claims: "You are not just what you think you are; you are more sublime. . . ." But before we look at who we really are, who is it we *think* we are?

Most of us identify with our two outermost bodies. When we identify with our physical body, we feel we are man or woman, American or Indian, old or young. When we identify with our subtle body, containing our thoughts and emotions, we feel "I am a Democrat" or "I am a writer," "I am a Christian" or "I am a Jew." Even better, we love to combine these identifications. We think: "I am a fifty-five-year-old Indian actress" or "I am a thirty-seven-year-old American writer."

The problem with these identities is that they are, at best, temporary and superficial; at worst, unreal. In the waking state I may be a writer, but in my dreams tonight I could be a thief. And in the state of dreamless sleep I'm not aware that I exist at all. So who am I? Really?

And as if that weren't confusing enough, these surface identities are constantly changing. Next year I will be a thirty-eight-year-old American writer. If I move to London the year after that, give up my writing and citizenship, and take up golf, I'll be a thirty-nine-year-old British golfer, and in my dreams God only knows who I'll be.

And yet, despite all the roles we play and all the changes that our minds and bodies undergo, there is a part of us that remains the same—untouched and unaffected. We call it "I." This perfect "I" is the same in everyone. It is the core of our personality and of all the little selves that populate the world. It is the peg on which all of our minds and bodies are hung. It lives inside us, within our bodies and our minds, but is detached and unaffected by them. This "I" may appear to be a laborer or a mother, smart or dull, a Hindu or a Christian, depending upon the body with which it is associated; but it, in fact, remains untouched, neither changing when our mind changes nor dying when our body dies.

Actually, we all know this. We know we are not our body and mind, since we say "*my* body," "*my* mind," the way we say "*my* house" and "*my* car." But whose mind and body is it? Who is that One we really are?

Yoga says we are the Self, the perfect and unchanging "I."

THE LIGHT OF CONSCIOUSNESS

There is another way, the yogic scriptures say, this Self may be described. "The Self is Consciousness. The Self is the Witness of the other three states."[2] This Self is the inner Knower, the One who illuminates our mind and understanding, the One who watches all our thoughts and deeds. A Christian mystic was hinting at this when he said: "The One you are looking for is the One who is looking."

A children's song describes it this way: "He knows when you are sleeping, he knows when you're awake, he knows when you've been bad or good, so be good for goodness sake!"

This is a good description of the inner Principle. It is the ever-present witness that experiences the states of waking, dream, and dreamless sleep. When we go to sleep it stays awake, and in the morning reports to us the substance of our dreams. Even in the state of dreamless sleep this inner witness is awake and watching the void. Like a person sitting up all night, staring at the test patterns on a television, it tells us in the morning we slept deeply, we saw nothing, no dreams appeared on our inner screen.

And when we do dream, it is this Principle that gives light to our dreams. Consider this: It's a moonless night. We go to bed, turn out the lights, shut our eyes, pull the covers over our head, and go to sleep. And suddenly, though it is pitch-black both inside and out, we *see* ourselves performing the actions of a dream. From whence cometh this dreamlight? What inner sun illumines the landscape of our heart?

Gurumayi Chidvilasananda, in a talk in New Orleans on February 2, 1985, described an extraordinary experience of this inner light which she had had the night before:

> There was just that light. I was trying to turn the light off, but there was light—bright, bright light. In my sleep, the switch was next to me and I could turn it off;

and I tried to turn the switch off, but the light wouldn't go off. And then there was this little voice that said, "Hey! Where are you? You think you can switch this light off according to your will? This is the light that shines in the moon and this is the light that shines in the sun. This is the light that gives light to all lights. You cannot switch it off." It was so bright! I said, "I must go to sleep! This is the light that gives energy to the waking state. This is the light of everything, it is the light of everyone." So, all night, I lay there looking at it.

SATCHITANANDA

So far I've described the Self as the source of our joy, our being, and our consciousness. Put these three together and we have one of the classical definitions of the Self. For while the yogic scriptures say this Self cannot really be described, when forced to do so they call it *sat-chit-ananda*.

Sat is absolute Being. Something that is sat is everywhere at all times. Though Henry Kissinger may have been in Cairo yesterday, Jerusalem today, and Washington tomorrow, he is still not sat, since he has not been in all those places (and everywhere else) simultaneously from the beginning until the end of time. Everything that *is* has its seat in sat, the way every wave has its existence in water.

Chit is absolute Consciousness, total knowledge. Chit knows everything that ever was, is, and shall be—plus everything that isn't, wasn't, and won't. Look at chit this way: once, as a child, you got a pebble in your shoe. You picked it out and threw it away. Chit knows where that pebble is. It knows where it will be forty years from now, in four hundred years, in four hundred and forty thousand. It knows what the inside of a pumpkin looks like before it's broken open. It remembers the sunset of the evening before you were born and knows the color of your granddaughter's eyes—though she won't be born for another sixteen years. Though you've forgotten them, chit remembers every detail of every dream you had in 1983. Chit.

Ananda is all the joy in all the worlds. It's the joy of angels as well as dogs. It's infinite and never-ending joy, so that if all the joy that each creature has felt since the universe began was rolled into a ball and dropped into ananda, that ball of joy would disappear, like a drop in the ocean.

According to yoga, this is the Self: sat-chit-ananda—absolute Being, absolute Consciousness, and absolute Bliss. Stranger still, yoga claims we *are* that Self.

THE HUMAN CONDITION

But how can that be? If we're the Self, then why don't we *feel* like it? How, you might ask, can I talk about all the joy in all the worlds when human beings suffer the way they do? For the fact is, we suffer terribly. The multiple terrors and agonies of existence do not overwhelm us only because most of the time we keep our eyes resolutely shut against them. Through all sorts of ruses, with all sorts of medicines and devices, we try to deny or ignore the depth of our pain and that of our fellow creatures, for if we didn't, we would go quite mad. We need not look to the Holocaust for examples of human suffering, either. Simply, honestly count and measure the frights and alarms that have befallen your own poor heart—the fears of childhood, the insults and rebuffs of adolescence, the anxieties and countless hurts and losses of later years.

Forget absolute knowledge and your granddaughter's eyes. What about the abysmal ignorance in which men and women live? Where do we come from, who are we, and where are we going? We have no idea, though we might depart at any moment.

And as for sat, being, most of us feel that our identity and existence is so much less than it could have been. We wanted to be a great concert pianist, but . . . alas, we ended up working as a clerk in a bank—and truth often seems as remote and unobtainable as some brilliant distant star.

Perhaps in the end, for most of us, it is the goad of our suffering, and not our high ideals, that turns us toward the spiritual path. For the scriptures insist that only when we penetrate to the core of our being and experience ourselves as sat-chit-ananda, uniting with our own inner Self, will our pain and misery end. However, they also say, because we really are that Self, even now while living on the surface of our being, commuting among the states of waking, dream, and dreamless sleep, we *do* experience the Self—but in a small and limited way.

We experience being, "I"-ness, but not absolute Being. Instead of feeling great and one with everything, we feel we belong to a single little mind and body, time, and place.

We experience consciousness, but it's not absolute Consciousness. Instead of being omniscient, we know only certain things and not others.

Instead of feeling a constant torrent of bliss, we experience spurts of pleasure and shocks of pain.

It is not that we don't experience the Self. It's just that our experience of our Self is restricted and small.

So what is it that keeps us from experiencing our Self in all its glory all the time?

Yoga says it is our mind.

CHAPTER 2

THE MIND

O the mind, mind has mountains; cliffs of fall
Frightful, sheer, no-man fathomed. Hold them
cheap
May who ne'er hung there.

—Gerard Manley Hopkins

Once while I was working as a bartender in New York City, a fellow came in, ordered a beer, and started to watch the Yankees game on the television in the corner. The TV was on the blink, the reception was bad, but the Yankees were winning—which in that particular bar was all that mattered. So I was surprised when the guy turned to me and said, "The Yankees look lousy."

"What are you talking about? They're winning, aren't they? It's like twelve–nothing."

"Yeah, but look at them," he said. "They're all wavy. Look at Reggie. He must be sick. His face is green!"

I looked at the fellow very carefully. The great thing about New York gin mills is that anyone can walk through the door—and does. Also, a lot of people have a peculiar sense of humor and like to try it out on bartenders. But this guy wasn't kidding.

Making no sudden motions, I snaked out my hand and took away his empty mug. You do that first before you eject someone. Otherwise, they just might throw it at your head. "That's the TV," I said very quietly. "That's not the Yankees."

"What are you talking about?" the guy said. "TV's fine. It's the Yankees who are screwy. Look, now it's snowing. In the middle of July!"

I looked at the television. A white electronic flurry was interfering with the picture. "That's not real snow," I told him. "That's just the reception."

"Hey, whatta you?" the guy said. "Mr. Know-it-all?" He was getting nasty.

"C'mon," I said. "Time to go."

"It's not me who oughta be leaving!" the fellow told the other patrons. "It's him!" he said, jerking a thumb in my direction. "And them damn Yankees!"

Of course, as the fellow left, everyone gave him a round of applause, for it was obvious the poor guy was mad. He was crazy because he did not understand that he wasn't really watching the Yankees at all, but only a series of electronic blips and images projected upon a glass screen.

And yet the yogic scriptures say that most of us make this same perceptual error—for when we look at the world we think we are seeing reality, when what we're perceiving is only that image of the world which appears in our own minds. And what this image looks like depends a lot upon our own inner television set and mental reception.

Thus, when our mind is upset we see the world in one way, while when we're in love we see it in quite another. To say the world *is* the way we happen to be feeling at the time is like saying the Yankees are wavy when the reception is bad.

It is for this reason the yoga scriptures say, *ya drishti, sa srishti,* or "The world is as you see it."[1] It is our mind, not the world, they say, that is the source of all of our experience: honor or dishonor, happiness or sorrow, bondage or liberation. Because this is the case, it is a mistake to believe that someone or something else is the cause of our pleasure or our pain. To attribute our happiness, or lack of it, to our husband or wife, boss or kids, national policies or the international situation, is to delude ourselves. Yoga says our happiness is not determined by the events, possessions, or people in our life, but by our mind.

Baba recalled a man who was brought before his own Guru, Bhagawan Nityananda, on a stretcher. The man was drooling and staring vacantly off into space. This man, they were told, was one of the richest and most powerful industrialists in India: he had thousands of employees, many factories, servants, houses, and cars. But recently he had suffered a nervous breakdown—his mind was gone—and now he could command no one and enjoy nothing.

The fact is, no matter how many possessions or blessings we have, we cannot enjoy them unless our mind is still and strong. A weak and restless mind will always warp our vision of things and sabotage our happiness—the way an untuned television makes the picture look bad. And yet the inverse of this unhappy axiom is also true: for yoga says, since the condition of our mind determines our picture of reality, we can become happy and completely fulfilled not by changing the world—but by changing our mind.

A SIDDHA'S MIND

Swami Muktananda was a perfect example of this. He was in a state of constant bliss. And yet it wasn't that he inhabited a perfect world. He lived and breathed in the same world as I did, sometimes in the same room. But because he possessed a perfected mind, his experience of the world was very different from my own. The same people that made me crazy gave him great joy; the heat of

India that I found so oppressive and draining filled him
with an experience of his own magnificence and power;
thunderclaps delighted him while terrifying me. A yogic
scripture describes this supreme state precisely: "Whatever is seen, heard, or felt, in every sense-impression,
nothing inauspicious is found."

THE HUMAN MIND

For most of us, however, this is not the case. Our mind
frets and worries constantly—even when absolutely
nothing is wrong. As Baba liked to say, "Give your mind
half a chance and it will always come up with a problem." And, I might add, this one little problem will take
over the whole of our mind. A thousand things may be
right in our life, but if one thing is "wrong," we're misera-
ble.

Just the other morning I was standing on the corner of
Eighty-sixth Street and Broadway when an ambulance
rushed by me without its siren on. To be perfectly honest,
it missed me by several feet, but it came close enough to
make my heart skip a beat. What had happened? Nothing
really. All I actually felt was a little gust of wind. But
then my mind took over. It went like this:

"My God! That ambulance almost ran me over! Why
didn't it have its siren on? If I had stepped off the curb
another foot and a half, it would have hit my leg and
knocked me over. And there I'd be in the middle of
Broadway, with a broken leg, struck by an ambulance.
Well, the ambulance would have to stop, of course. It's an
ambulance, after all! They'd load me in the back of it and
take me off to . . . what's the closest hospital around
here? St. Luke's! They'd call my doctor, of course, and my
mom. . . ." I saw my doctor and my mother looking
down at me with great sympathy and sorrow. And I knew

then the leg could not be saved. For an instant I felt a sickening fear. There I was in St. Luke's Hospital about to lose a leg, run over by an ambulance on Broadway. What a way to go!

Then I looked around me and realized I was not in St. Luke's Hospital at all. I was still standing on the corner of Eighty-sixth Street on legs that were perfectly intact. The ambulance had long since vanished. My trip to the hospital had been purely imaginary. The resultant pain and suffering, however, were very real. I looked at my watch. I was late for an appointment. I wondered what my client would say. My client was a difficult person and I began to have an unpleasant argument with him in my mind. "Where have you been?" he growled. "Don't give me that," I yelled back in my mind. "My God! I was almost hit by an ambulance!"

So it goes, for most of us, day in and day out. We don't control our mind, and so our mind runs us ragged. And our mind does this not once in a while, but hundreds and thousands of times a day.

For this reason, many yoga scriptures talk more about stilling the mind than they do about the Self, God, the Guru, or anything else. It is not that the human mind is evil or bad—only that, in most of us, it is totally out of control. The poet-saint Bhartrihari writes:

> *O my mind, my friend,*
> *Because of your fickleness,*
>   *I descend into hell.*
> *Because of your unsteadiness,*
>   *I ascend into heaven.*
> *The ten directions cannot contain you.*
> *And yet, never once, even by mistake,*
> *Do you think of the Self within.*[2]

THE THOUGHT-FREE STATE

"Yoga is the stilling of the thought-waves of the mind."[3]
This classical definition was first put forth by Patanjali in
the *Yoga Sutras,* the foremost work on yoga and the mind,
more than two thousand years ago.

Paraphrased in simple English, the *sutra* says: Yoga is
not thinking. *Not thinking!* Such an idea seems vaguely
shocking and downright un-American. Even as a child I
had a sign in my room that said THINK!—and all my teachers urged me to do it for as long and as hard as I could. If
I didn't think, I'd be stupid, wouldn't I?

Yoga says no, that just the opposite is true—that the
thought-free state is one of *more* consciousness, not less.

In other words, the scriptures say, if we didn't think all
the time, we would be free; for it is our very thoughts
which are our chains and which keep us from experiencing the bliss and power of our Self. This screen of
thoughts reduces our vision and conceals the Self the
way clouds in the sky obscure the light of the sun. Most
of us, as Gurumayi has said, "Become so fascinated by
the light streaming through the clouds, the light that
forms so many beautiful patterns and shapes, that we
forget the source of the light itself."

And yet, pretty as these patterns are, our most glorious
fantasies eventually become wearisome—while even a
momentary break in these thoughts allows a ray of divine
sunshine through. Artists call this "inspiration," a welling
up of insight from a deeper source; other people experience it as "intuition," a word that means literally "an
inner teaching"—as though there were a teacher hidden
inside us.

MATRIKA

But how exactly does our mind hide the Self and distort our picture of reality? What are these inner clouds made of? Yoga says, words.[4]

The scriptures explain it this way: In the depths of our being, subtle sounds are constantly arising. These sounds cannot be stopped. They are born as naturally and inevitably from within our being as the sky forms clouds or the ocean, waves. These sounds arise and join together inside us to create words, which in turn form thoughts, which in turn create mental images to which we respond emotionally. Depending upon whether the thought is good or bad, we experience pleasure or pain. If I think, "That ambulance almost hit me," I feel fear and pain. But if the same experience prompts me to think, "Boy, I'm fast. I got out of the way of that one!" I feel relief and pleasure.

Of course the same process is occurring in other people's minds as well. Letters and words arising within them become thoughts and images which spill out as speech, enter our ears, and carve out a meaning and feeling inside us. If the letters come together to spell "Idiot!" we feel one way; if they combine to create the phrase "I love you," we feel quite another.

Yoga calls the power inherent in this ever-rising stream of inner sounds *matrika*. Matrika means, literally, "the unknown Mother," for it is she who sits in the depths of our minds and is the source and creatrix of all our experience. She comments on everything that happens and whispers to us the story of our lives, like a grandmother telling an endless fable. Sometimes her words make us angry, sometimes they make us laugh, sometimes they make us worried, sometimes they make us smile.

But all these feelings, good and bad, are based upon the ceaseless stream of the *matrika shakti*.[5]

LIMITED KNOWLEDGE

Because of this matrika, the scriptures make an extraordinary claim. The *Shiva Sutras* say: *Jnanam bandhah*, "Knowledge is bondage."[6] To western ears this is a heretical thought. Most of us have been taught to believe that just the opposite is true, that knowledge is freeing, that learning and education invariably lead to our greater good.

Yoga agrees. With one caveat. It says *true* knowledge is liberating, yes, but *limited* knowledge is not. In fact, it is our limited knowledge that prevents us from experiencing the Truth. Explaining this, Muktananda writes, "Knowledge can be pure or impure. If you think, 'I am a sinner. I am in bondage. This is my caste' . . . you are under the influence of impure knowledge. Pure knowledge arises when the Guru's grace sets you on the path of Siddha Yoga. The inner Self is revealed, followed by the awareness, 'I am He.' Then one identifies oneself with the whole cosmos, feeling, 'I am indeed everything. I alone pervade everywhere, within and without.' This is the highest state."[7]

In other words, if we truly knew and felt in our bones we are the Self, that our nature is absolute being, consciousness, and bliss, that we are the immortal and eternal witness of all temporal things, certainly such knowledge would make us joyous and free. But the "knowledge" that most of us live with is a very different kind indeed. Instead, *we know that we are not the Self.* We know that we are Joe Schmoe or Suzy Schmoe from Secaucus, New Jersey, and we feel our mortality and imperfections keenly. We know we are good at chess, but have a lousy singing voice and only nine hundred and forty-two dollars in the bank; that our dog is nice and our boss is mean; and that the rent on our apartment is going up twenty percent come the first of the year. We know there are many things we want and many things we need and many things we will never get and many things that can harm us, and that someday we will die along with everyone we love—and steeped in this impure knowledge, we lead the greater portion of our lives. No wonder we're unhappy!

Even in our dreams this ceaseless stream of subtle inner words keeps manufacturing all kinds of images, desires, and fears. Only in the state of dreamless sleep, when our consciousness goes beyond our mind, does the voice of the matrika fall silent, and we experience peace. It is this false, limited, impure "knowledge," based upon the flow of inner words, that yoga calls "bondage."

MUNDANE METHODS OF STILLING THE MIND

Yoga says true knowledge, real happiness, and lasting peace come from a place beyond the mind, a source deeper than our thoughts. Only when our mind is still and clear, and the ceaseless stream of inner words is stopped, can this knowledge, peace, and happiness be tapped. It's not that we have to attain the Self. We have only to still the thought-waves of our mind and there the Self will be, like a treasure glimpsed on the floor of a windless lake. For when our mind becomes still, the blissful inner Self automatically flashes forth and we experience its joy and peace.

This is not a yogic secret. Everyone knows this already, whether consciously or not. No one wants worries. No one likes a clouded and agitated mind. Everyone knows they feel happy when their mind is clear and still.

The question, then, is *how* one goes about stilling the mind. Apart from deep sleep, which is almost everyone's first choice, the second most popular way to quiet the mind is by satisfying its desires. Since the mind becomes agitated when it wants something, and momentarily peaceful when a desire is fulfilled, most of us expend our energy attempting to satisfy the desires of our mind. This, by the way, is the great allure of wealth. It is not that people want money in and of itself. We want it because it promises the instant gratification of all desires—and with it, mental peace.

So why don't we try to become millionaires, then, instead of yogis? Because this solution doesn't work for very long. If it did, there would be no need for yoga. While it is true that the mind becomes still when a desire is fulfilled, it is only for a moment. Then another disquieting desire arises. And another. And another. Also, there are many desires we can never fulfill, try as we may. If the only thing that will make us happy is to become President of the United States, most of us are probably out of luck.

The truth is, the mind can never be satisfied by giving in to its desires. This is because the mind, by its very nature, is insatiable. The more we give it, the more it wants. And if we allow the mind to have everything it fancies, it will take us upon a terrible journey, an endless chase after this and that, like a man pursuing a wild and tireless pony.

Liquor and drugs are another way to momentarily still the mind, and people use them for this reason. However, to work effectively, their doses must constantly be increased—and when their effects wear off, we suffer cruelly.

Entertainment and art are more salubrious and sophisticated means. Sometimes the mind can be tricked or moved or shocked into stillness. This last is what gives horror movies their allure. Why else would people pay good money to watch maniacs cutting up bodies with buzz saws, or mummies rising from the dead? Because at that moment, when the coffin opens and the monster's scaly hand appears, the mind stops, and in that instant, bliss wells up from deep within—a bliss so delicious we scream aloud. Special effects, roller-coaster rides, surprises of all kinds work on the same shocking principle. Hurtling through space in a rickety cart sixty feet above the ground, our mind is "blown," and the joy of the Self flashes forth.

Art and beauty still the mind through more exalted means. I remember the moment I finished *War and Peace.* I had been reading it all summer and had seen and felt so much—so much life, so much death. And for a moment, as I closed the book, my mind stopped and I was flooded with a sense of such serenity and peace—a peace that passeth all understanding, as God must feel looking down upon His creatures.

Beautiful landscapes have a similar effect. A commentary on the *Vijnana Bhairava,* a yogic text of one hundred and twelve *dharanas,* or techniques to experience the Self, declares: "When by contemplating any scene— vast, awe-inspiring, deeply moving—the mind is thrown into a state of ecstasy and mute wonder, and it passes into the thought-free state, then that is the moment when suddenly and instantaneously the Supreme Reality reveals itself."[8]

In all these instances we've used external means of one sort or another to still the mind and *experience the bliss of our own inner Self.* This is a crucial understanding. For yoga insists that the joy we receive from all these things—roller-coaster rides, nature, art, monster movies, food, and sleep—is always there inside us waiting to be felt. If the joy were really coming from the object itself— from the book or the sunset—then everyone would feel it equally whenever that object was encountered, just as anyone who comes in contact with a radioactive substance receives a dose of radiation. But joy is not like that. Put one acquaintance of mine on a roller coaster and she throws up, while monster movies bore her. But give her a bowl of popcorn and a soap opera and she's in heaven. For it is *these* things that still her mind and allow one brilliant beam of that inner joy to stream forth.

YOGA

The scriptures say there is another, more successful way to still the mind and to liberate the joy within: through yoga. Once we understand the mechanics of joy, we can dispense with all these messy and external means to procure it. If joy is within us, why do we need to carry around a thousand-page Russian novel to get it out? Why pay six dollars for the dubious privilege of watching a maniac with a chain saw chase screaming schoolgirls through the Halloween night in order to feel a little thrill?

Why not go directly to the source of our bliss? Why not still the mind with the most powerful and effective means at our disposal, so that we feel that happiness and peace all the time? This is the aim of yoga, and of its principle practices like chanting and meditation. Gurumayi says: "By the annihilation of various thoughts, you come at last to the perfect I-consciousness, the Self."

Baba Muktananda was a prime example of this attainment. He had permanently stilled the stream of inner words. And even when thoughts did arise in his mind, because he was anchored in the Self, he did not identify with them and so they did not bind him. Nor was he seduced or hurt by the sounds that arose in other people's minds and issued from their lips.

Many times I saw people praise Baba, several times I

saw them curse him. While he responded appropriately to what they were saying, their words had no effect upon his inner state. You could not make him feel bad by telling him you didn't like him. Similarly, you could not make him feel any better by telling him he was great. Somehow, he had overcome the power of the matrika. He was established in the Self.

This inner state was so potent and pervasive that simply to go near to him was to find oneself affected. In his company, my thoughts would often stop automatically and I would glimpse for an instant the thought-free state in which he lived. It was extremely sweet: pure and blissful. The physical world looked sharper, fresher; sense-impressions were keen and unfiltered. And as I came near him, I would find myself uplifted by the power of his state far beyond the thoughts of my mind. It reminded me of the first time I ever flew in a plane, and the wonder I felt as the plane lifted up through the gray, dirty weather. For there—lo and behold—the sky was blue! And the cabin was bathed in radiant sunshine.

CHAPTER 3

THE WORLD

The world is a means to God.
It is not an obstacle. Why do you hate it?

—Krishnasuta

Once upon a time, two demons were terrorizing heaven. Even the greatest of the *devas* were powerless against them. In panic, the gods fled, taking refuge at the feet of Lord Vishnu. They appealed to Vishnu for relief and shelter.

Vishnu appraised the situation and, through his power of yoga, saw that the demons had been granted a boon by Lord Shiva whereby they could be slain only by each other. Since they were brothers and fond of each other, this was unlikely. So Vishnu transformed himself into a beautiful and ravishing woman named Mohini. This alluring creature then appeared before the two devils and batted her eyes.

The first demon said, "Marry me!"

The second said, "No. Marry *me.*"

Mohini looked at the two loathsome creatures, whose mouths were smeared and caked with blood, and said, "Hey, what kind of girl do you think I am? I can't marry both of you. I'll marry the one who's the strongest and most powerful."

Instantly the two demons set upon each other to see who would win Mohini's hand. The reverberations of their contest shook the universe: the sea sloshed from its bed, the sun fled into the netherworld, and the moon, which had always been romantically pale, turned a shade paler. For days and nights the battle raged. The devils clawed each other's faces and gouged each other's eyes. They ripped each other's throats; they bit each other's necks. Whenever one of them began to tire, Mohini would simply wink at him, and the battle would resume. At last both devils exhausted themselves and collapsed, dead at her feet.

Mohini, having accomplished her task, now made a fatal mistake. She looked at herself in a pool of water and thought, "My, what a beautiful woman I am. No wonder those monsters wanted my hand." And intoxicated with her own beauty, she sauntered off, regarding her reflection in every stream and pool. In fact, she soon forgot she had ever been Vishnu. She believed she was Mohini and she felt that such a beautiful woman was deserving of a husband. And so she approached the great Lord Shiva and offered to be his wife.

Shiva agreed to marry her, proposing they have Brahma, the Creator, wed them.

But when they approached Brahma to perform the ceremony, the hoary deity looked aghast. He said to Mohini, "You can't marry Shiva!"

"And why not?" Mohini asked.

(And here, anticipating the punch line of a story he had already told a thousand times before, Baba would start to laugh so hard, the tears would stream from his eyes.)

"Because—you're *Vishnu!*"

And yet, as with everything he did, the humorous fable served a higher end. For Baba would always conclude by saying Mohini's forgetfulness and predicament are our own. Like Mohini, we are God, but we believe that we are not. Like Vishnu, we are the Self, the Lord of the Universe, yet because of our mistaken identification with our body and mind, we think we are a beautiful woman— a writer, a subway conductor, or a mother of three.

How did this backward transformation come about? How does God forget who he is and become a human being? A yogic text explains: *"Chiti,* or universal Consciousness, descending from the Absolute, contracts to become the mind. Because of this contraction, She becomes an ordinary being, subject to limitations."[1]

Or, in simple English, God, by limiting his powers, becomes you and me.

GOD AS YOU

Once a person asked Baba, "When you look at a tree, do you see God in it?" Baba answered: "I don't see God *in* the tree, I see God *as* the tree." Similarly he tells us, "God dwells within you *as* you."

For, according to both Baba and the scriptures, God did not create us the way a carpenter creates a house—out of some material very different from himself. Rather, God, the Self, or universal Consciousness (whichever you prefer), *creates us by becoming us,* the way gold becomes a bracelet or an actor assumes a role.

And yet even when God becomes us, he still remains God—just as a golden bracelet is still gold, or Sylvester Stallone, while playing the role of Rocky or Rambo, is still Sylvester Stallone.

The *Shiva Sutras* say: "The Self is an actor."[2] For according to the Siddhas, all the creatures of this world are different characters played by a single actor, God.

THE SELF IS THE STAGE

But these same sutras go even further. Not only do they say "The Self is the only actor," they say, "The Self is the stage on which the drama takes place"![3] It is the Self that has become this world and everything in it. Or as the great Siddha poet Jnaneshwar says:

> *A wall painted with a picture remains a wall.*
> *Likewise, the Supreme Principle remains Itself*
> *While appearing as the Universe.*[4]

But how, you might ask, does divine Consciousness do this? How does it become baseball diamonds, TV dinners, literature, the sense of touch and smell, rhododendrons, carpenter ants, airplanes, and your brother's mustache? Jnaneshwar explains:

> *When He appears before Himself in different forms,*
> *Consciousness becomes a Seer,*
> *And what appears is called the Seen,*
> *The way a face in a mirror*
> *Becomes an object of perception.*
>
> *He creates the Seen out of his own Being*
> *And shows it to Himself.*
> *In this way, there appears the triad*
> *Of the Seer, the Seen and Seeing.*
>
> *But just as in a ball of string*
> *There is nothing but string,*
> *Inside and out,*
> *Understand that this triad is not three.*
>
> *A face which is alone*
> *Sees itself in a mirror,*

And as it looks, the act of seeing
Naturally occurs.

O Famous One, in the same way,
Consciousness,
Without dividing,
Appears to become three.

Understanding this is the secret of everything.[5]

Did you ever want to know the secret of everything? According to Jnaneshwar, this is it. This universe of billions of different objects, actions, perceptions, and creatures is in reality a single Being—the way all the different worlds, objects, and characters in a dream are not in any way different from the dreamer. It's as though Vishnu became not only Mohini, but the demons, the heavens, the sun and moon, the terrified devas, and the pool that held his face.

CONTRACTION—CREATION

But in order for the Self to become us and this universe, it first has to, on one level, temporarily limit its powers and forget who it is.

Think about it. If the Self were aware it was everywhere at once, it couldn't be different people. If it knew it was God, it couldn't pretend to be a sidewalk, apple cider, you and me. If it knew it was omniscient, there would be no need for universities, students, or teachers. No need for books, detectives, or astrologers, either. If it felt its bliss all the time, why would it do anything?

So the Self voluntarily contracts its powers, the way a tortoise pulls in its limbs, or a healthy young actor pretends for a couple of hours to be a crippled old man. The Self is still the Self. It still has its powers intact inside itself, but in order to play the game called the universe, it chooses, for a while, not to display them. And when I use the word "game," I'm not being facetious. This is what the scriptures call it: either a *vilas,* a play, or a *lila,* a game.

And then, like most of us, the Self gets so caught up in the excitement of the game, it appears to forget who it is.

This can happen quite easily. Once, in prep school, I was invited to a friend's summer home. It was during the Kennedy era, and we played a game of touch football. I was at the time a rather dim-witted long-haired athletic young thug. On the opposing team was the diminutive wife of a network anchorman.

Though it was just a game, of touch no less, it got more and more exciting and intense. Finally my friend made an end run. I was supposed to block for him. As the petite wife of the anchorman tried to tag him, I launched myself at her with a flying cross-body block. I took her *out*— believe me. I must have knocked the poor woman twenty-five feet. Ten minutes later she was still lying on the ground, only semiconscious, with people huddled all around her, and everyone looking at me like I was some kind of jerk—which I was.

Eventually she recovered and was helped off the field —and though she was not seriously hurt and most graciously forgave me, for the rest of the weekend I was the goat. People kept asking me, "Why did you decimate her like that?" And my only answer was, I got excited. I forgot who I was, I forgot who *she* was. I forgot, you see, that it was only a game.

According to yoga, this is our predicament precisely. The universe is really a game or play enacted by us, the Self. But having entered the game and assumed our various roles, we've forgotten who and what we really are, and have temporarily lost much of our power. Suffering from this cosmic amnesia, we take our lives and selves in deadly earnest. Every time someone leaves the game, we weep. When a new player enters—we hand out cigars.

PLAY OF CONSCIOUSNESS

Based on this view of the world, the Gurus of Siddha Yoga, unlike some sages, do not deny the existence of the universe or maintain that the world is illusory or unreal. How could it be? The world and all the beings in it are God himself, albeit in a contracted and nearly un-recognizable form.

Because of this understanding, Siddha Yoga sees the world as a "play of Consciousness." This vision was so central to Baba's experience that he made it the title of his spiritual autobiography, *Chitshakti Vilas,* and gave the same name to his successor, Swami Chidvilasananda.

But what is the nature of this play of Consciousness which is the universe? According to yoga, its nature is Self-revelation. The universe is God revealing himself to himself. As Jnaneshwar says, "It is Consciousness alone which becomes the Seer, the Seen, and Seeing."[6] It's like a peacock looking at his tail, or a pianist amazing himself by playing piece after piece from his enormous reper-toire. To put it another way, God, disguised as us, looks out through our eyes and sees himself in the form of the world.

When we look at a sunset, for instance, it is the Self revealing to itself its own beauty; when we see a puppy or a baby, we are the Self experiencing how cute and adorable we are. A thunderstorm displays to the Self its own magnificence and power; a silent night reveals to it its serenity and peace.

But why, if the Self is eternal and unchanging—and the

Self is the world—is the world ever-new? Again Jnaneshwar explains:

> *Innumerable forms and sights arise,*
> *But it is the one pure Consciousness*
> *Which is the substance of them all.*
>
> *This one underlying Consciousness*
> *Is so intoxicated by the glory of its vision*
> *That It does not like to see Itself*
> *In the mirror of the universe*
> *Wearing the same jewelry twice.*
>
> *It has so much wealth that*
> *It causes Itself to appear*
> *In a different form at every moment.*
>
> *Once they are created,*
> *It regards the objects of the world*
> *As boring,*
> *And so, It shows Itself*
> *Ever new and freshly-created sights.*[7]

KARMA

But though, according to yoga, the universe is only a sport or play of God, this game has strict, impartial rules. One of these rules is the universal law of cause and effect, known in the East as *karma*. The law of karma states that for every action there is corresponding reaction.

The other morning, while I was jogging on Riverside Drive, I saw a mugger steal a woman's purse. He grabbed the bag, pushed the woman down, and ran about twenty-five yards before he was tackled by two beefy joggers, who instantly whipped out handcuffs and two-way radios and placed the thief in the back of a van. The "joggers," it turned out, were plainclothes policemen.

Now, no one would say that the mugger was arrested by chance. Though I was running right behind him, no one arrested me. What I had witnessed was cause and effect: instant karma. The thief performed an action, robbery, and immediately received its karmic fruit: arrest and incarceration.

But what if the thief had gotten away—as so many do? What if he had taken the money from the woman's purse and gone on to live happily, or criminally, ever after? In this case there would be a crime, but no apparent punishment.

Well, we shrug, life is unfair. And this is how most of us view the world. We believe in karma, but only to a limited degree. If we throw a rock at a plate-glass window, we fully expect to hear the sound of breaking glass, but if we cheat someone or betray their trust, we think that somehow, some way, we might just get away with it.

But the Siddhas tell us this can never be. Just as in the physical world there can be no action without an opposite and equal reaction, so in the moral and metaphysical realms this same truth prevails. *All* actions bear fruit. What fools us into thinking otherwise is that different karmas take different lengths of time to ripen.

In the natural world, we know this to be true. Not every action produces an immediate effect. Rain falls on copper and nothing appears to happen, but over the years, exposed to the weather, the copper takes on a beautiful turquoise patina.

We may stick our hand in fire and suffer at once, but if we are exposed to certain toxic chemicals, our symptoms may not manifest for years.

In the same way, a person may commit actions that do not appear to bear fruit, but yoga insists this is not the case. These actions, it says, will bear fruit someday, and if not in this lifetime, then in another.

REINCARNATION

All the apparent inequities and injustices in the world are instantly resolved when one accepts the reality of karma and its inevitable corollary, reincarnation. Why is one child born healthy, another one lame? Why is one student brilliant, another one slow? Why does one person have an interest in meditation, another in politics, a third in art? Why is one artist talented, and another not?

Environment, some people answer. The stars. Nutrition. Genes. Fate. But all these answers beg the question. Why is one person born into a rich and nourishing environment and another into deprivation? Why does one person have healthy genes and another have genes that bring about his downfall?

Chance, we say. But yoga says there is no chance. Yoga says *everything* is the effect of a previous cause. The circumstances in which we're born, how long we live, and the conditions of our life are the result, not of chance but of our previous actions.

In some cases, this is obvious. We've all known people whose actions in this life have shortened or prolonged it: the alcoholic who drinks himself to death, or, conversely, who stops drinking and miraculously recovers. And yet there are many events that are inexplicable in terms of actions committed in this one lifetime: the innocent child who is hit by a car, a good person crippled by a savage disease, an honest, hardworking man or woman who loses all he or she has in some natural disaster.

And yet yoga says the only reason these events seem unjust and inexplicable to us is that we don't see their cause—which is hidden by the curtain of a previous life.

It's like a soap opera on television. If you tune in one week, you might wonder why Alex is so poor and Harriet so wealthy. But if you had watched the show the week before, you would know that Alex is poor because he gambled away his inheritance and Harriet is wealthy because she scrimped and saved for years. Similarly, yoga says this life is only the latest episode in a long and nearly endless melodrama.

Of course, it isn't necessary that we *believe* in reincarnation to pursue yoga. I certainly didn't when I began. It was only later, after I started meditating regularly under Gurumayi's guidance, that I came to accept reincarnation as true.

Once, in deep meditation, I saw a big burly man in a top hat and cape, carrying a doctor's satchel and limping beside a river that I knew to be the Mersey. This man was a doctor and he had spent his life rendering service to the poor. I also knew this man was me in a former existence, and as I came out of meditation I understood at last the answer to a dozen minor mysteries, from my avid interest in medicine as a child down to the slight turn in my left foot with which I'd been born—all that was left of a once terrible limp. I understood why, at the age of seventeen, I had spent the summer as a social worker in the slums of Liverpool. I also understood why, at the end of that summer, I had been invited to Buckingham Palace to be thanked personally by the Queen Mother. Until then it had always seemed to me an inexplicable quirk of fate that what little good I had done that one summer had been so royally rewarded. But after that meditation I understood that the honor I had received was not for that one summer alone, but for a whole previous lifetime of selfless service. All actions bear fruit. There can be no cause without an effect. I had not been rewarded in my former life, so I had to be rewarded in this one.

THE WITNESS

But how, you might ask, does the law of karma reward and punish us like this?

The empowerer of the law of karma is the Self, and the very nature of the Self is chit—universal Consciousness. The Self sees everything and *remembers it.* There is no action so secret, ancient, unconscious, or small that is hidden from it.

Baba used to tell of the Guru who gave each of his two disciples an apple and told them to go eat it where no one would see them. The first disciple went into the jungle, hid behind a rock, waited until it was night, then ate the apple with great secrecy. The second disciple wandered for days, then returned to the Guru with his apple uneaten. The Guru, feigning anger, asked him why he had not followed his command.

The disciple answered, "O Guruji, I tried to obey you, but whenever I was about to eat the apple, I myself saw what I was about to do."

This ever-present witness is the Self. In the West, we call it our conscience. According to yoga, it watches all our actions, good and bad, and impartially presents us with their fruit. It is for this reason the saints enjoin us to be vigilant and perform good actions, for, as Gurumayi says, "We never know what action we have committed in the past. We never know when that action will rear its head and say, 'Hey, remember me?' "

THE WHEEL OF SAMSARA

But according to yoga, liberation is not simply a matter of being good. Even our good actions keep us in bondage. The scriptures liken existence to a great wheel: on it, they say, all the creatures in the universe revolve, performing actions and receiving their fruits. Good actions produce higher births, bad actions lower ones.

Even our human body is the result of our good actions. Did you really think it was dumb luck you were born on Long Island as a human being while some other soul just happened to be born as a dung-beetle in the Kalahari Desert? The great poet-saint Namdev says:

> We are finally reborn
> as human beings.
> It is only at the last turn of the cycle
> we get a human birth.
> If we miss our opportunity,
> the cycle repeats itself . . .
> Know the inner Self
> in this very body.
> Look after it very carefully—
> or you will have to come again.

This cycle is called the ocean of *samsara*, the wheel of birth and death. In the West, we tend to think of life as great. But from the yogic perspective, an unenlightened life is sorrowful and full of pain, since even the highest birth entails a vast diminution of our divine powers.

How is it, then, we got into this predicament; how did we become bound to this wheel? Again, like Vishnu, a.k.a. Mohini—by forgetting who we are. All of our problems, the Siddhas say, arise from the ignorance of our essential nature. Because we think we are not the Self, we feel imperfect. We then feel we need this and we lack that, and so we begin to perform various actions—to attain some things and to avoid others. In this way we become embroiled in karma.

This, according to yoga, is the real tragedy of the human condition. The Self, having forgotten who it is, com-

mits action after selfish action which keep it chained to
the wheel of rebirth. A person is born, reaps the fruit of
his karma, and dies, only to be reborn and die again—
and again, and again, and again, in an almost endless
and unstoppable round. Good actions may get us into
Buckingham Palace, but even they will not free us from
the wheel.

Is there no way out, then?

Kabir, standing in a marketplace, watching a millstone
grinding wheat, comprehended the terrible enormity of
this cycle and asked this same question. He saw that all
beings, including himself, would be crushed like grains of
wheat by the terrible wheel of time. In fear and trembling
he began to weep. A wandering dervish, seeing him dis-
traught, approached and asked him the reason for his sorrow. Kabir, pointing at the grinding wheel, cried that he,
too, would be ground up like so much grain.

Then the holy man asked the miller to stop the wheel
and to raise the upper stone. He pointed to the stick that
connected the upper and lower stones and showed Kabir
how the grains which adhered to the stick were intact.
Then he said, "O Kabir, this stick is the Guru Principle,
around which the whole universe revolves. If you want to
be freed from the grinding stone of time, you must find a
Guru and stick close to him."

Kabir asked where he might find such a being. The dervish said: "In Benares there is a great Guru named Ramananda. Go to him. Only he can save you from the wheel
of birth and death."

How does the Guru save us? By showing us who we
really are. By telling us, "You are not Mohini, you are God
himself. Great and divine light exists inside you!"

For in the end it is only our ignorance that binds us, the
chains of words inside our minds. Because this is the
case, it's not that we must become something different;
we must become only who and what we truly are. Baba

says, "If you could 'attain' the Self, you could also lose it. By doing yoga, you attain nothing—except the realization that you are the Self and that the Self is already attained."

This is not an intellectual realization. It's not like suddenly remembering the capital of Brazil. It's like being *in* Brasilia, eating the food and drinking the water.

And so now, like Kabir, having seen the painful alternatives, let us set off in search of a Guru.

CHAPTER 4

THE GURU

The Guru is not different from the conscious Self.
Without doubt, this is the truth, the truth.
Therefore, the wise make an effort to seek him.

—Guru Gita

One of the things that attracted me to Harvard as an undergraduate was its motto: *Veritas,* Truth. Perhaps I was naive, but I sincerely believed I would discover the Truth behind its ivy-covered walls. But though many good people there spoke about the Truth, researched it, wrote papers on it, read about it, and questioned it, no one I met seemed to have actually *experienced* it.

After a while I began to feel like a hungry man who wants a bowl of ice cream—and gets a history of the dairy industry instead! Experts tell him the price of ice cream and what it's made of. Still others claim that thousands of years ago, in a land far away, people actually tasted ice cream and wrote books about it, describing it as sweet and cold. But I didn't want to know *about* ice cream. I wanted to eat some.

It was this same desire for the Truth that first attracted me to literature, I think, for sometimes, in fiction, I glimpsed the Truth for a moment or two. At college, I studied writing with the great American novelist and short-story writer Bernard Malamud. In one of his novels, *The Assistant,* there's a telling exchange about exactly this:

> *He asked her what book she was reading.*
> "The Idiot. *Do you know it?"*
> *"No. What's it about?"*
> *"It's a novel."*
> *"I'd rather read the truth," he said.*
> *"It is the truth."*[1]

The Truth, in other words, is not a piece of information. If it were, we could get it from a newspaper, an actuary, or a computer. The Truth is, first and foremost, an inner experience, and that's why it's sometimes glimpsed through art.

Unfortunately, even an artist through whom the Truth is flowing may not be experiencing it fully himself. We are all familiar with people who, like ladles that never taste the nectar they serve, nourish the entire world while their own souls go starving.

In the end, even great art is not enough. I knew a man who hanged himself in a room filled with Rembrandts. Potent and lovely as art and literature are, they cannot redeem a false and unexamined life, nor can they serve as a substitute for actual experience—just as we cannot taste ice cream through the medium of words.

In the same way, we cannot attain the Self merely by reading, hearing, or thinking about it. This is the bailiwick of literature, art, philosophy, and religion. To have a lasting and life-transforming *experience* of the Self, yoga says, you must approach a Guru.[2]

THE NEED FOR A GURU

Ironically, it is precisely this which is a stumbling block for many seekers—for if Westerners flee from the word "philosophy," they foam at the mouth at the word "Guru." And yet Muktananda's words have the ring of hard-won truth when he writes: "You cannot attain the Self through your efforts alone. If anyone thinks that he can, then I can tell him he is wasting his time. I spent forty years of my life wandering, thinking I would attain the Truth by myself. Only after forty years, when I met my Guru and began to listen to him, did I attain something."

Nor is this only Muktananda's experience, or that of seekers in the yogic tradition only. A Greek Orthodox text, the *Philokalia,* states:

It is necessary to seek a teacher
  who is himself not in error
  and to follow his instructions.
If there is no such teacher in view,
  one must search for one, sparing no efforts.[3]

Rumi, the great Sufi master, writes:

Do not rely on your own skills and footsteps. . . .
Whoever enters the way without a guide
  will take a hundred years
  to travel a two-day journey.

Finally, Jesus' words "I am the Way, the Truth, and the Life" and "No one comes to the Father, but through me" may be read less as a declaration of his unique place in history than as a reaffirmation of the Guru's eternal role.

THE ETERNAL GURU

The Guru is not an individual, then, but an eternal, cosmic Principle. Just as God's power of *maya,* or illusion, conceals our true nature and deludes us into thinking we are something other than what we really are, so another power of God, called "the Guru," dispels our ignorance and reveals to us our true Self.

> *The syllable* gu *is darkness,*
>   *and the syllable* ru *is light.*
> *The Guru therefore is the supreme knowledge*
>   *that swallows the darkness of ignorance.*[4]

This power is primordial and universal; it has been operating in all places since the beginning of time. While it is above and beyond all temporal things, it exists inside each one of us as well.

> *The Guru Principle moves and moves not.*
>   *It is far as well as near.*
> *It is inside everything*
>   *as well as outside everything.*[5]

Even if there were no human Gurus, there would still be the Guru: "God is the Guru of even the most ancient of Gurus."[6]

But though this Guru principle exists within each one of us, it cannot easily be accessed, except through contact with a Guru in human form. This is a subtle but crucial point. For while the Guru is *not* an individual but a divine power inherent in us all, a human Guru acts as the channel for this power, the way an outlet gives us access to electricity. It doesn't matter how many volts of electricity we may have coming into our house; without an outlet, it's useless. The *Kularnava Tantra* puts it this way:

> *Though there is surely milk in the cow,*
> *   you must get it from her udder.*
> *In the same way, though God is everywhere,*
> *   His grace flows through the form of the Guru.*

For this reason, the *Shiva Sutras* say, *Gururupaya:* "The Guru is the means."[7] Another Shaivite scripture says, "The Guru is the grace-bestowing power of God."[8]

When this grace enters our life it does amazing things —not the least of which is that it reveals to us our true divine nature.

> *One should perceive the inner Self*
> *   through the gift of the Guru's grace.*
> *By this path of the Guru,*
> *   knowledge of one's Self arises.*[9]

MEETING THE GURU

Finding such a master, then, is of primary importance to a seeker on the spiritual path. But how does one go about this?

In a way, there's nothing for us to do. The Guru comes into our life when we are ready to meet her and not before, or, as it is said: "When the pupil is ready, the master appears." And often most unexpectedly, I might add.

I know a man who spent years traveling from one holy place to another in India, looking for a master; then, disillusioned and exhausted, he returned to California, only to meet Baba at a gas station half a block from his home. Many other seekers who are not in the physical proximity of the Guru first see her in their dreams. This is quite possible, since, as we have seen, the human Guru is really an outer expression of the inner Guru principle. When this principle wishes to reveal itself to us, it takes the form of a human Guru in order to appear to our sight.

Because this Guru principle is beyond time and space, it can appear to us at any time or place. An elderly Japanese man recalled how as a child he had gone to church with his parents. During the service he had had a vision of a beautiful woman in red, and at the sight of her, he said, he had felt the presence of God very strongly.

Fifty years later, in a Tokyo auditorium, he saw a photograph of Gurumayi dressed in scarlet robes. At the sight of her picture, he burst into tears, for he recognized her as the red-clad being in his childhood vision—though Gurumayi had not even been born at that time.

Such a mystical experience leaves one with an unshakable faith in the Guru's authenticity, nature, and power. But for many of us, the Guru does not enter our life in quite so dramatic a fashion. In that case, how can we tell if a Guru is for real?

QUALIFICATIONS OF A TRUE GURU

My father is a dedicated consumer. Before he purchases anything of value, he researches the product thoroughly. Frankly, if people were as careful about choosing a Guru as my father is about buying a toaster-oven, there wouldn't be a problem. But when it comes to spiritual teachers, many people are either irrationally paranoid or unbelievably naive. If someone calls himself a Guru, they accept him without question or reject him out of hand without, in either case, examining his credentials.

Both approaches are dangerous and shortsighted.

There is a saying in India: "Filter your water before drinking it and examine a Guru before accepting him." This is sage advice. Certainly there are charlatans, cranks, and frauds in every field—from business and finance to art and science—and spiritual life is not immune. So be sensible. Just as you would choose a college only after checking its accreditation or a bank only after first reviewing its assets, so you should choose a spiritual teacher with care. After all, with a bank, it's only your money you're investing, while in the case of a spiritual teacher, you're entrusting him with your immortal soul.

For this reason, the same yogic scriptures that insist on the need for a Guru frame strict criteria for choosing one. A teacher who meets these qualifications is called a Siddha Guru or a *Sadguru*.

I explained this once to a friend of mine who was meeting Baba for the first time. Afterward, my friend remarked, "For such a sad Guru, he looked pretty happy to me." Sad, of course, doesn't mean "unhappy," but true. It comes from sat, which is Truth or absolute Being, that supreme principle which exists everywhere at all times. The first qualification for a Sadguru is that he or she must be completely one with this Principle. This is only common sense. After all, if the Guru doesn't know the Truth, how can he impart it to you? Can a person who doesn't know the capital of Brazil tell you what it is?

While such great souls are admittedly rare, they have appeared at times in all religious traditions. In the East they are called Siddhas, in the West they are called saints. Because these beings actually embody the Truth, they teach as much by example as by words.

A disciple of the Baal Shem Tov, a great saint of the Hasidic tradition, was once asked what his master taught.

The disciple replied: "I don't go to the master to listen to his teachings, I go to watch him tie his shoelaces."

This is because everything the Guru does is divinely inspired, every action he or she performs teaches and reveals the Truth. The *Shiva Sutras* say of such a being, "Even his casual words are mantra; knowledge of the Self is the gift he bestows on all."[10] A commentary concludes: "The mere sight or touch of such a yogi can free one from the cycle of samsara."[11] This is the inestimable value of a Siddha Guru.

Second, it is said, the Guru must have full knowledge of the scriptures. This is more than an intellectual knowledge. It is the knowledge that springs from being merged in That which all the scriptures attempt to describe. Gurumayi recalls:

> *Around Baba we got to see a lot of scholars. And when they came to Baba they would be so dry, but spilling out verses from the Vedas and other philosophies. Finally, two hours later, they would ask Baba, "Have you anything to say?" And Baba would say, "No." And they couldn't understand that. They would ask him, "Didn't you study the scriptures?" And Baba would say, "Yes." "And you don't have anything to say?" "No." And they would keep looking at him because they couldn't understand that. And as they looked at him, they would become quiet and still inside, completely silent within themselves, and they would have an experience then of that Truth contained in the words of the scriptures.*

THE LINEAGE

The third qualification of a true Guru is that he or she must come from a spiritual lineage of Gurus, and be made a Guru by his or her own Guru.

In other words, like produces like. Doctors teach other

people to become doctors, lawyers make lawyers, cats make kittens, and apple trees bear apples, not figs. Similarly, a person becomes a Guru when he or she is made a Guru by a Guru, who in turn was made a Guru by his own Guru, and so on back into time. This line of spiritual power is known as a *lineage*. Just as kings and thoroughbreds have bloodlines, so a Sadguru must come from a bona fide line of spiritual teachers. In other words, a Guru is not born, but made.

For this reason you cannot wake up one morning and declare yourself a Guru. You can, of course, but what does it mean? You could just as easily declare yourself a brain surgeon—but I certainly wouldn't let you operate on me.

THE SIDDHA LINEAGE

According to tradition, the lineage of Siddha Yoga derives from the first Guru, Shiva. This name denotes Supreme Consciousness and is not to be confused with Shiva, the third person of the Hindu trinity.

In the course of time the lineage is said to have passed to Vasishtha, who was the Guru of Lord Rama, and eventually to the sage Vyasa, to whom are attributed many great works of spiritual literature, including the *Mahabharata*. From Vyasa, the power of the lineage was eventually passed down to the world-renowned spiritual teacher Shankaracharya, who lived around 800 A.D.

In modern times the spiritual power of the Siddha lineage was embodied in the person of the great Indian holy man Bhagawan Nityananda. His successor was Swami Muktananda, who, five months before he passed away, named Gurumayi Chidvilasananda as his spiritual heir.

Again, for the discerning, the lineage reveals the true nature of the Guru. The scriptures say, "The Guru is not the *vyakti,* the individual, but the *Shakti,"* the spiritual power that flows through that form. Many of us had a direct experience of this truth when Baba passed away, and we began to experience the same spiritual force that had flowed through him flowing through Gurumayi. Baba had left us—but the Guru had not. The Guru had simply taken up residence in another body.

THE GURU'S TOUCH

As we have seen, a Guru must be permanently established in the Absolute, must be learned in the scriptures, and must come from an authentic spiritual lineage and receive the power of that lineage from his or her own Guru. But all these qualifications only lead up to the final qualification: A Guru must be able to give direct knowledge of yoga and an experience of the Self. This is the Guru's main task; if a Guru can't do this, he's not a Guru.

Before I met Baba and Gurumayi, I had the notion that a Guru taught yoga in much the same way that Mrs. Kern taught me typing in seventh grade.

Mrs. Kern was a brilliant typist. She could type eighty words a minute without an error. I, on the other hand, typed as if I were wearing mittens. And it seemed the more I practiced, the worse I got.

Some days when it was going rather badly, I used to wish that Mrs. Kern could somehow, just by touching my fingers, impart to me her power of typing, so that suddenly I would be able to type as brilliantly as she.

Fantastic, you say! And yet this is what a Siddha Guru does. A Siddha Guru does not simply teach the science of yoga in an intellectual way. A true Guru gives us an immediate *experience* of it by imparting to us her own inner power and spiritual state.

All the yogic scriptures agree on this vital point. The *Kularnava Tantra* says:

> *A person is eligible to become a Guru*
> *when through his touch*
> *a disciple experiences Supreme Bliss.*

The *Vayaviya Samhita* states:

> *Knowledge of yoga and an experience of the Self*
> *arise instantaneously*
> *from the Guru's touch, word, or look.*

This is an extraordinary claim—and not one you are expected to believe without proof. I know it is true only because on October 30, 1979, in a small apartment on the Upper West Side of Manhattan, it happened to me.

CHAPTER 5

THE POWER

When Kundalini awakes,
all doors are thrown open.
God reveals Himself in the heart.

—Swami Muktananda,
Mukteshwari

October 30, 1979 in New York was a spectacular day of bright fall sunshine and cool blue shadows. At eleven that morning, coming home from a meeting, I stopped in at a bookstore across the street from Columbia University. The moment I walked through the door my attention was arrested by an extraordinary face staring at me from the dust jacket of a book. The face was so radiant and serenely beautiful that I went over and picked the book up. Its title was *Play of Consciousness;* the face, I discovered, was that of its author, Swami Muktananda.

I had never heard of Swami Muktananda, but, intrigued, I bought the book and headed home. There I took the phone off the hook, sat down on my couch, and began to read it.

As soon as I did, I started to have the most peculiar reaction. First I began to laugh; then I began to cry. Then I began to laugh again. It wasn't that the book was humorous or sad; rather, my emotions seemed to have gone out of control. Soon I came to a chapter called "The Greatness of the Guru." There I read, "The true Guru awakens the disciple's inner Shakti and makes him revel in the bliss of the Self."

The instant I read those words I felt an actual physical tap, three times, in the space between my eyebrows. Then something like a spring made out of light uncoiled at the base of my spine, shot up my back, and exploded ecstatically in the crown of my head. A wondrous surging energy began to course through my body, accompanied by wave upon wave of bliss. It was like falling in love without an object, and so I just kept on falling, falling. . . . The next thing I knew, I had jumped off the couch and had begun to twist and stretch and bend my body, moved by the inner current of power. I couldn't understand what I was doing, or why. I thought it was some kind of spiritual gymnastics, and then a voice inside me said, "This is yoga."

With that understanding I sat down on the floor and, though I had never studied hatha yoga a day in my life, my legs knit themselves into the half-lotus posture, my hands formed different gestures, or *mudras,* and a variety of breathing techniques, or *pranayama*—which I had also never studied—automatically occurred. After a while, these various movements ceased, and my mind, breath, and body became extremely still as I fell into a state of deep meditation. It was the most exquisite mental state my mind had ever known, like a bull's-eye of concentrated power. Three hours later, when I came out of meditation, I felt transfigured. A revolution had taken place inside me and I was full of a sublime and vivid joy.

How can one explain this amazing experience?

In a modern experiment the truth of the ancient yogic scriptures had been confirmed once again. The Siddha Guru, Swami Muktananda, by virtue of the spiritual power inherent in his words, had given me knowledge of yoga and an experience of the Self. He had given me this experience through a classical transference of spiritual energy known as shaktipat.

THE DESCENT OF GRACE

Shaktipat means, literally, the "descent," *pat,* of *Shakti,* "power" or "grace." Baba writes: "For countless ages Shaktipat has been used as the secret means of initiation by the great sages. Concisely, to transmit one's own glory and luster of divine enlightenment into the disciple and give him an instantaneous direct experience of Brahman, the Eternal Spirit, is the secret meaning of Shaktipat."[1]

Furthermore, this experience, I soon learned, was not to be a one-shot affair. This influx of Baba's power had permanently activated my own latent spiritual energy, known in yoga as the kundalini. The principle here is not unlike that of one candle lighting another, or, to use a more modern analogy, like using jumper cables to start a car. The power from a stronger engine is used to ignite the weaker one. Once started, the second motor runs on its own.

And that's exactly how I felt—as if a switch had been thrown and my spiritual engine had been set into motion. The Self, which up until that day had been just a fuzzy concept to me, now became a living experience, a physical force. At all hours of the day or night I could feel an actual stream of energy flowing up my backbone. And in the weeks that followed, my life was totally transformed. Habits I had had for many years fell away. I stopped eating meat and smoking cigarettes and I began waking up at four in the morning with an irresistible desire to meditate. I saw brilliant lights of different colors. Sometimes when I sat to meditate, the sound of *Om* arose in me spontaneously, or I would find myself performing strenuous hatha yoga postures—the full-lotus, the bow and the locust poses, even shoulderstands!

I stress that this all happened to me spontaneously, inspired by the inner Shakti, without any previous knowledge of yoga or any conscious thought on my part.

KUNDALINI SHAKTI

What exactly is this extraordinary energy called kundalini Shakti?

According to the scriptures, this cosmic energy has two aspects: gross and subtle. On the gross level, as we have already seen, the whole world is its embodiment. A Shaivite scripture states:

It is divine Consciousness alone,
  luminous, absolute, and free-willed,
  which flashes forth
  in the form of countless worlds.[2]

In other words, God goes on an adventure, disguises himself, and becomes the world. He does this through his Shakti, or creative force, which in yogic mythology is sometimes pictured as his consort or feminine aspect. It is this Shakti, or creative energy, of Shiva—the unmanifest and unchanging aspect of the Absolute—which appears as the sun and planets, lakes and mountains, which grows as trees and fruits and grasses, and which grazes in the form of cows. It is this same divine energy which manifests as time and space, night and day, hunger and desire—and which has become both me and you.

And yet the scriptures say a curious thing. They say that while Shiva and his Shakti may appear to be different, they are, in fact, one.[3] Shiva is in no way separate from Shakti, just as water does not exist separate from its wetness, or as fire is not different from its power to burn. If it's wet, it's water; if it burns, it's fire. There's no way anyone can separate the two. The same is true of God and his creation, of Shiva and his power to create.

And yet God and his creation certainly *appear* to be different. The tree outside my window does not look at all like Shiva, nor did I feel much like him when I woke up this morning.

This is because the gross, outer aspect of this divine creative energy conceals its true nature from itself. This is maya, ignorance, illusion, the "world-bewilderer." The scriptures liken its action to Rama, his wife Sita, and his brother Lakshman walking single file along a jungle trail. Lakshman tries again and again to catch a glimpse of his big brother up ahead, but Sita is always between them, blocking his view.

This is how it is for most of us. Maya, the world, stands in our way of seeing God. And so instead of seeing divine inspiration at work in our lives, we see only blind happenstance, economic forces, and brute necessity. But this is just an illusion caused by the deluding power of this cosmic energy.

Thankfully, this power also has another, inner aspect, which, instead of concealing the divine nature of things, reveals the Face behind the mask, allowing us, when the masquerade is over, to recognize our true nature and once again return to God. This aspect of the Shakti is known as the Guru.

Once, on a fishing trip to the wilds of Maine, I asked a farmer for directions to a lake. He told me how to get there; then, frowning at the dashboard of my car, he said, "Theyah ain't no gas stations out theyah, fella. Shuah you got enough gas?"

I did a quick calculation. The lake was forty miles away. I had about three gallons of gas and got about twenty miles to a gallon. "No problem," I told him.

He just nodded. "Ayuh."

And it wasn't until I had finished fishing and got back into the car that I realized what that old farmer had been trying to tell me. I had enough gas to *get* there, all right. I just didn't have enough gas to get back.

God is not so foolish. He plans ahead. Having created the world, he leaves enough energy in the body of creation to allow the creation to eventually return to him. For this is what the kundalini Shakti is, the residual divine energy remaining in a human being after its creation that empowers it to recognize its true nature and return to God. This Shakti, which is not different from the Guru, is sometimes called *shaivamukha,* the face of Shiva, for only when this divine indwelling energy is awakened can we see through the mask of maya and recognize God's face, which is in fact our own.

THE ROYAL ROAD

The fact is that the kundalini Shakti wants to awake and return home, taking us with her.

> *The kundalini Shakti is always watching*
> *for opportunities to redeem her devotees*
> *from the cycle of birth and death.*[4]

While waiting, she sleeps in the center of the human body, coiled in the *muladhara chakra,* a subtle energy center at the base of the spine. These chakras, or centers, are not located in the physical body, but in the subtle body which interpenetrates the physical one. While we cannot see this subtle body, we are all familiar with it—since it is in this body that we experience our thoughts, emotions, and dreams.

Once this Shakti is awakened by the Guru, she begins

to arise and unfold, moving through a *nadi,* or channel, in the subtle body known as the *sushumna,* which corresponds to the spinal cord. As she ascends she pierces and purifies five more chakras located respectively at the base of the reproductive organ, at the navel, the heart, the throat, and the space between the eyebrows.

For this reason it is sometimes said that the spiritual path is three feet long: from the base of the spine to the crown of the head. Looked at in this way, it sounds quite "do-able," doesn't it? After all, the awakened Shakti only has to travel thirty-six inches; even if she crawls at a rate of one inch per hour, she ought to arrive there in a couple of days. Right?

Not quite. For, in most of us, the sushumna nadi is filled with obstructions. These obstructions are called, in yogic terminology, *samskaras,* a word related to the English scar. Samskaras are the little scars of past impressions, a record of everything we've ever done over the course of our previous 8,400,000 lives.

As the Shakti moves through the sushumna she encounters these past impressions and acts as a sort of divine Roto Rooter to expel them. The expulsion of samskaras is absolutely vital, since these old impressions keep our experience of reality limited and small. Moreover, it is due to the power of these samskaras that we are born again and again. The removal of these past impressions by the awakened kundalini is called a *kriya:* a purificatory movement of the divine energy. Kriyas may take the form of hatha yoga movements, or intense emotional states. The subject of kriyas is explored more fully in the chapter on meditation.

Finally, the rising Shakti, having purified the seeker, reaches the *sahasrara,* the thousand-petaled lotus, and stabilizes in this topmost chakra at the crown of the head. And it is here, in the supreme spiritual center of the human body, that the Shakti merges with Shiva and the process of evolution is completed as the seeker attains the highest goal of human life.

This final state is known by different names in different traditions. The Buddhists call it *nirvana,* or enlightenment; Christians name it sainthood, or union with God; the Sufis, *fana,* or passing away. In yoga, this supreme attainment is known as Siddhahood, Self-realization, or *moksha,* liberation, and it is said to be a state of eternal and unshakable joy.

THE MOTHER OF YOGA

But on her way to granting us Self-realization, the Shakti bestows many spiritual gifts. For in Siddha Yoga, it is not we who meditate, but the power of the Shakti, which stills our mind and draws us deep inside. In fact, all the practices and experiences we need for our spiritual growth come to us naturally and spontaneously through the inspiration of this divine force.

After shaktipat, the eight classical yogas may arise in a seeker in varying mixtures and degrees. One person may find himself drawn into deep meditation as in raja yoga, while another may engage in the selfless service of karma yoga. Intellectuals may experience an opening of their heart and emotions as in bhakti yoga, while emotional people may be flooded with a sudden understanding of scriptural ideas, as in jnana yoga. A person may see inner lights, as in laya yoga, or perform the movements and mudras of hatha yoga. All of these experiences may occur, or only some of them. In this way, Siddha Yoga is tailored for each individual soul. One size does not fit all. Everyone's experiences are different and everyone gets exactly what he or she needs.

For example: At an early point in my *sadhana,* or spiritual practice, whenever I sat for meditation, I would find myself touching various parts of my body—my heart, throat, head, and stomach—while intoning strange sounds such as *hrim* and *shrim* and *hum*. I did this spontaneously, urged from within by some inner Knower.

It was not until several years later, while I was studying *The Tantra of the Great Liberation*, an obscure yogic text, that I came upon an explanation of what I had been doing. It was a yogic technique called *nyasa*, in which the subtle body is infused with *prana*. The parts of my body I was touching contained chakras, or spiritual centers, while the sounds I was making were Sanskrit "seed-syllables," or mantras. I knew none of this consciously at the time it occurred.

Such wonders are explicable only when we bear in mind that the awakened Shakti is universal Consciousness. It is Shiva, the inner Guru, the all-knowing power of our inner Self. Using different spiritual techniques, the Shakti purifies and divinizes the body to make it capable of holding the highest state. Baba puts it beautifully when he states: "The Shakti Kundalini burns up the inner dross and incinerates it in the fire of yoga until the body is pure gold."

TRANSFORMATION

But along with spiritual transformation, the awakened kundalini transforms our mundane lives as well. This is very easy for the Shakti to do, since kundalini's outer aspect *is* the world. Many people find, upon the awakening of this energy, that dramatic improvements occur in their life: promotions, new opportunities, and the fulfillment of long-held desires. Speaking of the Shakti, Baba writes:

*She improves our daily life and makes perfect what-
ever is not perfect in our lives. . . . She will make you
able to look after your family in a better way and take
care of your business or profession more skillfully and
intelligently. She improves a student's memory and
concentration. She makes an artist a better artist, a
doctor a better doctor. . . . All talents, all inspiration,
all creativity, lie in the womb of the Kundalini, and
when She is awakened, She releases great creative
powers. There are people who after this awakening become great poets or compose significant philosophical
works. For some, Kundalini takes the form of Lakshmi,
the goddess of wealth, and they come into a lot of
money. In others, it takes the form of authority and
they become great leaders.[5]*

Sometimes, the changes may appear at first to be nega-
tive—but inevitably they are for our greater happiness
and good. For example, a man who had been plagued
with severe earaches all his life found, upon receiving
shaktipat, that he was spontaneously performing headstands while his hand struck repeatedly at the base of his
skull. To his horror, fluid began to drain from his ear. But
within a week, owing to this unique form of therapy, the
blockage was relieved and his earaches permanently disappeared.

Because the aftereffects of an awakened kundalini can
be intense and profound, some people are afraid of it, but
there is no reason for fear when the Shakti has been
awakened by a Siddha Guru. For in addition to awakening the Shakti, the Siddha Guru guides and controls it so
that its workings are entirely benign.

THE AUTOMATIC YOGA

Siddha Yoga, then, is a Self-propelled yoga. Once the kundalini is awakened our future is assured, since it is only a matter of time before it merges in the crown chakra, bringing with it liberation. How long this journey takes depends upon a number of factors—including the faith and intensity with which we pursue our spiritual practices, and the spiritual attainment we bring from our past.

In some rare, ripe souls, enlightenment may occur at the moment of receiving shaktipat. In most disciples, however, the process takes some time. Traditionally, the path of Siddha Yoga may be completed in multiples of three years. It took Baba nine years to complete his sadhana. At any rate, Baba says that even for the slowest disciple, liberation is guaranteed by the end of three lifetimes.

This may sound like a long time—but whether it is or not depends entirely upon our perspective.

One autumn day a seeker found a Guru sitting under a tamarind tree from which had fallen all but its three last leaves. The seeker asked the Guru how long it would be before he was liberated. The Guru pointed to the tree and said, "It will be as many lifetimes as there are leaves on this tree."

"Three lifetimes!" the seeker cried, and went away profoundly discouraged.

That spring, another seeker spied the same Guru beneath the same tree—only now the tree was in full blossom. He asked the same question and was given the same answer.

"Thank God," he said, delighted to know he would

someday be liberated. "After millions of births, what's another thousand lifetimes?"

CONCLUSION

As we have seen, the science of yoga is said to have first been revealed by the Lord of Yoga, Shiva, who passed it down through a lineage of Siddha Masters to the present day. Furthermore, it is said that the Guru and Shiva are one.[6] Such an attribution is difficult for many modern people to accept, especially if one considers Shiva to be a six-armed Hindu god who lives in heaven.

But this is not what Siddha Yoga means by Shiva. By Shiva, it means the Supreme Reality. As Muktananda says: "Shiva is neither Hindu nor Buddhist nor Christian nor Muslim. Shiva is your own inner Self."

In other words, Siddha Yoga doesn't come down to us from some god in heaven. Yoga is a *power* inherent in Shiva, the inner Self of all. When this power is awakened by a Siddha Guru, knowledge of yoga arises spontaneously from within.

Because the kundalini Shakti resides in every human being "like oil in sesame seeds, butter in milk, or fire in tinder,"[7] the awakening of kundalini is everyone's birthright and one we owe it to ourselves to claim. Gurumayi says: "As long as this power is dormant, we experience how bound and terribly limited we are. But once it is awakened, we experience such bliss. We come to know what this life is all about. We become totally one with the beauty of God."

Since the Guru is united with this inner energy, the Guru can very easily teach us from within. Once someone said to me, "Swami Muktananda has a lot of disciples. How can he give you individual instruction?" The answer is, very easily. Baba did not have to come to my apartment and give me personal instruction in hatha yoga, lessons in meditation, and lectures on Eastern philosophy. Instead, he awakened my inner power and the rest followed on its own.

This explains, perhaps, the plethora of yogic symbols and postures found in artifacts worldwide, from India to Yugoslavia, and from Denmark to Raccoon Creek, Georgia. Scholars ignorant of the workings of the kundalini Shakti have long argued over the probable routes of diffusion. Did Indian Gurus visit first-century America and teach the natives there the lotus posture? Or did early Danes visit India, stopping off in Yugoslavia on their return? How else to explain it? And yet these same scholars never ask, "Did the Greeks teach the Romans how to sleep?" or "Where did the Egyptians learn the art of dreaming?" For everyone knows that the ability to sleep and dream are inherent in every human being.

Similarly, according to the yogic scriptures and the teachings of the Siddhas—and as I myself experienced firsthand—yoga is a natural faculty inherent in Shiva, the Self of all. In most of us this power is dormant, but when conditions are right—that is, when an ardent seeker comes in contact with a Siddha Guru—a divine energy is awakened inside us. Then yoga, with its attendant postures, states, and practices—such as meditation, chanting, divine love, and spiritual wisdom—naturally and spontaneously arises. For this reason, Siddha Yoga is not Eastern or Western, old or new, nor can it be said to belong to any one country, culture, or tradition. Yoga is simply the name for what follows when we awaken the sleeping giant inside us all.

Part II
THE PRACTICES OF JOY

The King's *wazir* was in deep trouble. Meditating that morning, he had become so absorbed in his inner being that he had forgotten his morning meeting with the King. Now as he arrived at the palace gate, winded and out of breath, he discovered what he had feared the most. The sun was already high in the sky, like a red fist threatening the desert, while the King and his ministers were waiting for his arrival over cold tea with ill-concealed impatience.

The King asked, "Why are you so late?"

The wazir answered, "Forgive me. I was praying, Your Majesty."

"Praying," the King asked, raising his eyebrows. "To whom?"

"To God, Your Highness!"

This answer irritated the King. "You were sleeping," he said. "Admit it. I will forgive you."

"But I wasn't," the wazir replied truthfully. "I can't lie to you, my King. I was praying."

"And how," the King inquired, "can you pray to a being who does not exist?"

The wazir was shocked. "But he does exist, Your Majesty!"

"If he exists," the King said, "then show him to me."

At this the wazir's heart sank, for such a thing was beyond his powers.

"Tell me where he lives, then," the King said reasonably, "so that I may go and visit him."

But the wazir couldn't do this either. He only looked uncomfortable and bewildered.

The King sneered and, turning to his ministers, said, "And I rely upon this man to help govern my kingdom?" He looked at the wazir. "You idiot, get out. And don't come back."

The wazir left the palace and wandered into the desert. There he came upon a young boy seated by himself on a tiger skin. Though the child was alone, he seemed to be quite happy.

The wazir greeted the child and, in answer to the boy's questions, told him his sad story. The boy said, "Don't worry. I will answer the King's questions and get your job back as well."

So the boy and the minister returned to the palace. The wazir told the King that he had brought him someone who could answer his questions. The King and his ministers looked askance at the half-naked child, even as they waited for him to give them his wisdom. But first the child said that he was hungry, and demanded a glass of milk.

As soon as it was brought to him, he stuck his fingers in it, saying, "Where is it? Where is it?"

"Where is what?" the King demanded.

"Why, the butter, of course. You see, my mother told me there was butter in milk."

The King's patience was at an end. He was tired of these people. First the minister, now the wretched boy.

"O boy," the King said, "there is surely butter in milk, but you must first churn the milk to make the butter appear."

"O King," the boy said, "God, too, surely exists, but first you must perform sadhana, or spiritual practices, if you wish to see him."

THE ARMCHAIR PHILOSOPHER

Such advice may seem obvious. Everything else in life requires some effort, but when it comes to spirituality even the most intelligent people seem to become deluded and confused. I recently read the autobiography of a highly regarded English philosopher who said he had never found God. And yet it was clear from his autobiography that never once in the course of his ninety-odd years had he performed even the simplest spiritual practice.

The Siddhas tell us, God exists inside. If you don't go within, you won't see him. It doesn't matter how old you grow, how many books you read, how famous or holy you're considered, or how long you wait. It's like a man sitting in his backyard bemoaning the fact he has never found gold. One wants to ask him, "Did you ever *look* for gold? Did you ever go up into the mountains and pan for it? Did you ever go to Africa and dig for it in the mines? Gold does not grow on trees in New Jersey. It doesn't fall from the sky."

In the same way, to discover that Truth which is within our own hearts is the goal of yoga—and for this we need to perform spiritual practices.

THE PRACTICES

Every saint teaches differently. There are some saints who, like Bhagawan Nityananda, stay in one spot and speak through silence, while others like Baba and Gurumayi roam the globe, meeting millions and teaching tirelessly. In this next section I'll be sharing my experience of the techniques and practices of Siddha Yoga as taught by Baba and Gurumayi.

While Gurumayi draws upon a vast fund of knowledge, using stories and teachings from the saints of many different paths, the techniques and practices she recommends almost all come from the ancient Siddha tradition and can be found described precisely as she gives them in such texts as the *Vijnana Bhairava,* the *Spanda Karikas,* and the *Shiva Sutras.* In other words, these techniques are unadulterated and extremely pure.

For thousands of years they were secret as well, being passed by word of mouth from a Guru to a handful of close disciples. It is only in the last two decades, through Baba and Gurumayi, that these practices have been made available to the world at large.

On the other hand, Siddha Yoga is *not* about spiritual techniques. This great yoga is a spontaneous yoga that comes about through inner inspiration as a result of Guru's grace. Once awakened, the kundalini Shakti has full knowledge of the spiritual practices we need for our advancement, and automatically performs them whether we know how to do them or not.

We should bear in mind, too, that the practices are not aimed at attaining God. God, the Siddhas say, is *already* attained. The purpose of the practices is to purify the mind and break the chain of inner words, for when the mind is still and clear, the Self naturally reveals itself from within.

This is the goal of all spiritual practices—whether they be meditation, chanting, mantra-repetition, selfless service, study, or *satsang,* spending time in the company of saints. These practices purify the atmosphere within and without. In the end, however, God is revealed by his own light, or as the scriptures put it: "No means of sadhana can reveal Shiva. Can a clay pot illuminate the sun?"

CHAPTER 6

MANTRA AND CHANTING: THE VEHICLE

I do not dwell in heaven,
nor am I seen in the orb of the sun;
more than that,
I transcend the minds of yogis;
yet, O Pandava,
though I am lost to others,
I can be found in those
who chant my name aloud
with love.

—Jnaneshwar Maharaj

I: Mantra

When last we saw Kabir he was drying his tears in the marketplace, getting ready to go to Benares to find the Guru Ramananda. The only problem was that Kabir was a Moslem and Ramananda a Hindu, and in those days the caste laws were strictly enforced, so Kabir could not ask for initiation directly. Still, Kabir was determined not to end up like a kernel of stone-ground wheat. So he thought of a plan.

He knew it was Ramananda's habit to bathe in the Ganges at three every morning in preparation for his meditation on the Self. And so, one night, Kabir dug a hole in the steps that led down to the sacred river. There he secreted himself and waited.

In the predawn darkness, as Kabir had hoped, the great saint approached. When Ramananda reached the step where Kabir was hidden, he stumbled upon him, and in surprise cried out his mantra, *"Ram!"* Kabir leaped to his feet and said, "O Guruji, you have given me your mantra.

You have therefore given me initiation. I am now your disciple!" And with that, to Ramananda's amazement, Kabir ran off into the medieval night.

MAGIC WORDS

Every great adventure story has magic words, and the supreme adventure is no exception. In the tale of "Ali Baba and the Forty Thieves," the magic words are "Open Sesame." These words open the door of the cave where the jewels are hidden. While this device may seem like a bit of literary whimsy, it is, I suspect, the imperfect remembrance of an age-old spiritual technique—one that allows us to gain access to our own inner treasure. In yoga, the magic words that open the cave of the heart are known as mantras. And this is why Kabir was so ecstatic to have secured one.

A mantra, then, is the vehicle, the password, that allows us to enter and explore our own inner realms. It is also the armor which protects us from anything inauspicious we might encounter there.

The power of sound to alter our consciousness is a well-known phenomenon. From the shaman's drum to the works of Bach and Handel, to the gospel music I heard yesterday on the car radio, sound has been used in every age and culture as an avenue to the divine.

But a mantra is something else again. In addition to giving us a glimpse of the Self, it has the power to completely merge us with the goal. A mantra can do this because a mantra is not a sound or word that, like other words, was created by human beings. A mantra is God himself in the form of a word. *Mantra maheshwara,* the scriptures say: "Mantra is the Lord Himself." Or, as the Bible puts it, "In the beginning was the Word, and the Word was with God, and the Word *was* God."

THE SEER OF THE MANTRA

I once had the direct experience of this. One morning while meditating at Gurumayi's ashram in South Fallsburg, New York, I went to the very depths of my being and saw something I cannot describe, except to say that it was an expanse of pure Consciousness—without seam or shore or stain or end.

To say it *was,* would be a lie; to say it *wasn't* would be untrue. It was beyond name and form. To call it God would be to do it an injustice. It was neither dark nor light, and while it was empty it contained all things.

Then suddenly, out of this divine nothingness, I heard a sound. It was like a drum beat, or a heart.

And as the sound got louder, I recognized that it was the mantra, *Om Bhagawan.*

There is a technical term in yogic literature called the "seer of the mantra," but I had never understood it. I had always assumed that the mantras we chanted in Siddha Yoga had been composed by musical and literary saints. But the "seer of a mantra" is not the mantra's composer, but its hearer, its *discoverer!* The fact is, no human being composes a mantra. A mantra is the sound-body of the Self. And as we approach the Self in the deeper states of meditation, we can actually hear mantras and other divine sounds emanating from it, as I had heard the mantra *Om Bhagawan.*

The yogic sages, after listening to this inner music, realized that if they repeated these same divine sounds *when not in meditation,* the state of meditation could easily and automatically be induced.

This is the secret behind mantra-repetition and the reason why a mantra can so quickly and effortlessly unseal our inner doors. Mantra is the Word that was in the beginning, the cosmic sound-vibration that comes out of God. *Mantra svarupa*, the Goddess says: "Mantra is my very form."

THE CREATIVE POWER OF SOUND

According to the science of mantra, the whole universe is the emanation of mantra, the primal syllable *Om*. An Upanishad says: "The syllable *Om*, the imperishable Absolute, is the Universe. Whatever has existed, exists now, or will exist is *Om*."[1]

Since, according to yoga, it is this primal sound-vibration which has become all things, changes in the physical world can easily be effected through sound.

Certainly this is true on the most mundane level. By saying the words "Put this there" or "Place this here," I can make immediate changes in my physical environment. On a more subtle level, the mental worlds of Shakespeare's plays and of Tolstoy's novels have come into existence through a series of sounds. But this is sound's creative aspect. Sound also has the power to destroy.

DESTRUCTIVE SOUND

The first time I met Baba, someone asked him: "What causes mental illness?" His answer was a revelation. He said: "Bad mantras." I was living in New York City at the time, and for the next few months, whenever I passed a crazy person on the street, I listened carefully to what he was saying: "Jimmy don't love me. Can't find the fire engine! Where'd she go? Where'd she go? Somebody gotta get the priest. I told you I didn't do it! Kill him! He stinks!"

I listened in horror. These poor souls were chanting to themselves endless mantras of confusion and hate. And I understood then that these words and sounds were be-witching and destroying their minds—as surely as Ella Fitzgerald can spellbind you with her singing or shatter glass with her voice.

Nor is it only the mad who are hurt and wounded by sounds. If someone says "Idiot!" or "I don't love you," our whole being may become profoundly disturbed.

In the *Mahabharata,* the great Indian epic, sound is even used as a military weapon. Destructive mantras called *astras* are used by both armies to debilitate and terrify the enemy. The Bible describes a similar encounter: Joshua at the battle of Jericho . . . and the walls came tumbling down!

Other parts of the *Mahabharata,* along with many other literary works—the *Odyssey,* the *Iliad,* and countless fairy tales—recount how heroes and heroines are captivated and ensnared by spells.

This entrancing power of sound is remembered in our word *enchantment.* Obviously, an enchantment is brought about by *chanting* mantras—even if, west of the Indus, this fact has been forgotten.

Now, this "enchantment" may be of two kinds: destructive or creative, depending upon the character of the mantra from which it springs. If our mantra is "Everyone's out to get me" or "I'm such a worm, I feel so guilty," a state of madness or depression will surely ensue. Whereas if the mantra we sing is "I am Shiva, and this is all my glorious manifestation," the "spell" it weaves is luminous and divine.

MANTRA AS PROTECTOR

But not only does the mantra create and destroy, it sustains as well, as its etymology makes clear. The Sanskrit *man* is related to the Latin *mens* and the English mind; *tra* means "protection." A mantra, then, protects us when we hold it in our mind. I have heard many people tell of instances in which the mantra has protected them in muggings, car crashes, fires, and other calamities. But even greater than the physical protection it affords, the mantra protects our mind against its inner enemies: doubt, duality, desire, and delusion.

Just as fire is sometimes fought with fire, so we fight words with words. For nothing but the word of the mantra can vanquish the ceaseless stream of matrika shakti, which, arising inside us, screens from us our true nature and keeps us feeling limited and small.

LIVE VERSUS DEAD MANTRAS

The *mantra shastras*—the scriptures on mantra—claim there are more than seventy million mantras, and actually list several thousand. So why not simply peruse the list and pick a mantra that strikes our fancy?

Because the same scriptures tell us that in order for a mantra to be effective, we must receive it from a true Guru.[2]

It's a matter of authority. The same words have a different effect depending upon who says them. If a priest, a preacher, or a justice of the peace pronounces you and your beloved man and wife, you're married. If the milkman says the exact same thing, it means nothing. A prisoner cries, "Let me out, let me out," and the guards laugh. The warden says the same words, and the prison doors swing open.

Similarly, the mantra we use must have the authority of a spiritual lineage behind it; it must be empowered, enlivened, *authorized,* as it were, by a Guru. This is why Kabir had to receive the mantra from the mouth of Ramananda, who in turn had received it from his own Guru.

Nor is this empowerment of a mantra some meaning-less ecclesiastic ritual, but the infusion of an actual spiritual force. It is this potency or *mantra-virya* that makes the mantra work in us very quickly. The syllables of a mantra act as a vessel to hold this power. Such an empowered mantra is said by the scriptures to be *chaitanya,* alive. Without the Shakti behind it, a mantra is *jada,* dead. Such a "dead" mantra cannot bring liberation. It's like a cup with nothing in it: no matter how many sips we take, we will still remain thirsty; no matter how much we drink from it, we will never become drunk.

MANTRA REPETITION

The mantra may be repeated as we go about our daily chores. Some people use a *mala,* a string of beads, to keep them focused on the mantra. Even simpler is to repeat the mantra with every incoming and outgoing breath. This constant repetition of the mantra is known as *japa.*

Why would anyone want to repeat a mantra again and again? The *Maitri Upanishad* says: "What a person thinks is what he becomes. This is the eternal mystery. If the mind dwells upon the supreme Self, one enjoys undying happiness." A Christian mystic, Brother Lawrence of the Resurrection, names this same mental attitude "the practice of the presence of God."

This is what we are doing when we repeat the mantra. We are invoking the divine presence; our mind is dwelling upon the Supreme. With time, the energy in the mantra purifies and transforms the mind so that it sheds its doubts and limitations and returns to a state of pristine Consciousness. Until then, with the help of the mantra, our mind is not only focused on the Self, but it is *not* focused on all the thoughts and desires that usually tor-

ment us. The mantra quiets the endless stream of the matrika shakti, the little voice inside us that keeps us feeling
limited and small. Instead it gives us what Gurumayi
calls "an experience of the perfect 'I'-consciousness."

In order for the mantra to do this, however, the mantra
must be repeated with correct understanding. This understanding, the scriptures say, is that the mantra, the goal
of the mantra, and the repeater of the mantra are all one.
This means that we should not think of ourselves as different from Shiva or Shiva as being different from the
mantra. The mantra *is* Shiva in the form of sound, while
Shiva *is* our inner Self, who and what we really are. Contemplate this understanding as you repeat the mantra
and the mantra will do its work very quickly.

THE HOUR OF DEATH

But the yogic scriptures posit another and more sober-
ing reason for mantra repetition. They say that the moment of death has great significance. Whatever we remember at that instant determines our future birth. Now
it's all well and good to say that we will think of God on
our deathbed, but in actual fact, the Siddhas say, it is
extremely difficult to remember God at that time—especially if we've rarely thought of him during our lifetime.
For at death the mind reverts back to those thoughts and
images on which it continually dwelled.

An Indian shopkeeper thought he had figured out a
way to get around this problem: to remember God's name
on his deathbed without being bothered with ever thinking of him throughout his long and greedy life. He named
his three sons Shiva, Vishnu, and Brahma, all names of
God, and they worked together in the old man's shop.

When the hour finally came for the old shopkeeper to
die, he called to his first son, "Shiva!" Shiva came and

knelt by his father's bedside. Then he called out the name of his second son, "Vishnu!" Vishnu came and took his father's hand. A moment later, with his dying breath, he called to his third son, "Brahma!" Brahma dutifully appeared at his side. The old man looked at his three sons standing there before him. "Who's minding the shop?" he asked—and died.

Mahatma Gandhi, on the other hand, died with the name of God upon his lips. Like Kabir's Guru, Ramananda, he was so addicted to repeating his mantra, *Ram,* that nothing could shake him—not even an assassin's bullets. When he was shot the first time, he cried, *"Ram!"* He was shot again. *"Ram!"* He was shot a third time. *"Ram!"* he said, and closed his eyes. Though his body was attacked, his inner state was unassailable. So a true saint dies.

II: Chanting

There is yet another way to utilize the protective and purifying power of a mantra. When a mantra is set to music and sung aloud, it's called chanting. This is a particularly sweet and effective form of mantra-repetition, and one that can be done alone or in a group. Silent mantra-repetition normally benefits only the person who does it, but with chanting, its benefits extend to those who hear the mantra as well. In fact, the scriptures say the benefits of chanting are so great that animals, insects, and even plants are enriched by the power of the sound.

Perhaps this is why the grounds and gardens around Gurumayi are always so fruitful and bursting with life. The earth is constantly watered with chanting, and the trees, the shrubs, the animals, the people, even the buildings, seem to respond in kind. Everything seems more conscious, alive. Sometimes you can see the willows swaying in bliss, feel the buildings breathe, and see the marble courtyard bead with sweat in the heat of the summer sun. The fruits and flowers are magnificent around the ashram and twice the size of those a few miles down the road.

With such results it is no wonder, then, that Gurumayi continually emphasizes the power of chanting the divine name. Every Siddha Yoga program begins and ends with it. In fact, chanting is the most common spiritual activity that Siddha students do. Why such an emphasis on chanting?

The French physician, Dr. Alfred Tomatis, who studied the effects of sound on human beings, asked this same question and came to some remarkable conclusions. Joseph Chilton Pearce writes in *The Bond of Power:* "Tomatis speaks of 'discharge sounds,' which tend to fatigue, and 'charge sounds,' which give tone, health, and peace of mind. . . . Most chants come within the bandwidth for charging the brain."[3]

Tomatis also wondered, as many people do, why mantras are not chanted in the vernacular, in English, say, or in French. He discovered what various religious orders have known all along, that the benefits of chanting are enhanced when performed in one of the ancient "sacred" tongues such as Latin, Sanskrit, or Hebrew. Tomatis speculated it was because these languages are full of open vowels: *A-ve Ma-ri-a; Ha-re Ra-ma.* He concluded it was not so much the literal meaning of these phrases that had such power, but the very sound of the syllables, the vibrations themselves. For this reason they are untranslatable.

EXPERIMENTING ON YOURSELF

One does not need Dr. Tomatis, however, to appreciate the benefits of chanting. You can experience it for yourself by simply doing it. I've found that when I chant in the morning, my day goes well. Buses run on time, people are nice, animals are friendly. If I skip it, my day has another quality. Fires plague the subway, waiters spill coffee on me, and low-flying pigeons poop on my head.

At first I thought that chanting somehow changed the world. Then I realized it changed my mind. Since, as we have seen, the mind is the instrument through which we view the world, by changing the mind, our world view is transformed.

PURIFICATION

But it's not only the inner world that is affected by chanting. The outer world is cleansed and purified as well. Chanting prepares the ground for meditation. Baba says:

> *The main purpose of chanting is to bring about the purification of the entire atmosphere, internal as well as external. Through chanting the food becomes pure, even the plants and vegetables become pure and our inner hearts become pure. Chanting purifies the atmosphere, remaining present in subtle form, filling the sense organs and heart with divine vibrations. The result of the purity all around us is that we are able to meditate without any difficulty. So in order to destroy all the impurities and to become happy and joyful, we repeat the mantra and chant.*

This is more than the Beach Boys' "good vibrations," or the "positive thinking" they teach at midwestern sales seminars. The chants of Siddha Yoga are powerful mantras. Because they come from the Guru, they are infused with her spiritual force. Just as a doughnut dunked in coffee is saturated with coffee, so the syllables of the chants we sing are saturated with the Guru's Shakti and carry the Shakti's divine, transforming character.

TYPES OF CHANTS

Specifically, there are two types of chants that are sung in Siddha Yoga: *swadhyaya* and *kirtans.*

Swadhyaya means regular, daily recitation and study of the scriptures. This could be any number of texts from the *Shiva Mahimna,* a hymn to Shiva, to the *Bhagavad Gita.* The operative words here are *regular* and *daily.* The *Yoga Sutras* say, "Through swadhyaya comes the vision of your deity."[4] Baba says: "Swadhyaya embraces all aspects of yoga and grants all its rewards."[5]

The great daily session of swadhyaya in Siddha Yoga is the *Guru Gita.* Baba calls it "the one indispensable text." In the ashrams of the Siddhas, this "Song of the Guru" is performed early each morning without fail.

The *Guru Gita* is a most powerful *mantramala,* or garland of mantras. It brings both *bhukti* and *mukti,* worldly prosperity and spiritual liberation. Because there is no difference between a mantra and its deity, the *Guru Gita* *is* the Guru.

KIRTANS

Kirtans, or fast chants, are the names of God or of saints which are sung over and over. *Hare Rama* is a kirtan, as is *Jai Jai Muktananda.* Such chants are sometimes sung continually for as long as seven days and seven nights. This is called a *saptah,* which means "seven." The story of the saptah's origin points up the power of chanting.

A king was told he had a week to live. Naturally he

searched desperately to find some means to achieve liberation in so short a time. He considered meditation, austerities, and scriptural study, but all these practices took some time to give results. The only practice that bore fruit immediately was chanting. As the great Saint Tukaram said, "With the name of God on the lips, liberation is in hand." And so the king held the first saptah—a one-week crash course in liberation.

Chanting is also, for me at least, the quickest route to ecstasy. In fact, nothing I write can begin to describe the exquisite and blissful taste of these chants. The meditation hall is dark, lit by candles and with incense burning. Harmoniums and tambouras play. A lead group begins and the rest of the hall responds, calling the chant back and forth hour after hour, until time disappears. After a while, the voices sound like singing spirits, or like something you remember having heard once upon a time in some far-off heaven. And as you bathe in this ocean of mantras, rocking slightly with the current of the sound, you feel all the knots and tensions leave your body as wave after wave of love begins to bubble up within your heart.

LOVE

This is the real reason why we chant. Baba says, "Chanting the divine name is the most sublime way to develop inner love. The divine lover pursues God through the divine name."

Love is the delicious fruit of chanting. Chanting opens the heart, unblocks the springs of bliss, and makes love flow through every pore of the body. Chanting cools down the body, regulates the awakened Shakti, soothes the mind, and pleases the inner Power.

Many well-meaning people seek the Self through harsh

disciplines and strict austerities, but Baba said again and again that such asceticism isn't necessary. Just by repeating the name of God, just by chanting the mantra with love, we can dissolve all obstacles and attain all powers and realizations. The power behind chanting is the irresistible force that created the universe, so there is nothing in heaven or earth that can resist or oppose it.

A friend of mine once wrote Baba and asked him how she could be "blissed out all the time like you." Baba answered, "Chant the mantra with great feeling. Chant with all your heart and the bliss will come. No negativities can withstand the bliss of the Lord's name."

CHAPTER 7

MEDITATION: THE INNER JOURNEY

*Through meditation,
the Self is revealed.*

—Bhagavad Gita

Patanjali defined meditation as "stilling the thought-waves of the mind." Sounds simple enough. But try not to think for even one minute and you will quickly find that it is easier said than done.

For this reason, different spiritual traditions have offered a variety of meditative techniques to *zap* the mind and, in that instant, go beyond it into meditation. Chanting is one of them. Certain schools of *tantric* Buddhism employ visual imagery as well, while Zen Buddhists contemplate unanswerable questions, called *koans*. As our rational mind attempts to comprehend "the sound of one hand clapping," or to remember "our face before our parents were born," it stops—and we are taken beyond our mind into the thought-free state of the Self.

SIDDHA MEDITATION

Siddha meditation is an ancient and extremely potent way to still the mind and to access our inner Self. The

difference between Siddha meditation and other techniques is that instead of stilling the mind through our human efforts alone, we take the aid of a greater power, the
Siddha Guru and the awakened kundalini.

The result of this collaboration is a meditation that is
doubly powerful. For very little self-effort, we get extraordinary and immediate results. Baba used to say that Siddha Yoga is not "a yoga of credit" but a yoga of "ready
cash." By this he meant that you do not have to put in
long years of austerities and practice before you begin to
see results.

Nor is Baba's use of fiscal imagery frivolous, but scriptural. The Shaivite texts trace all of our problems to a
poverty of spiritual power. Siddha meditation ends this
impoverishment by allowing us to draw upon the infinite
spiritual wealth inside us and the power of the great lineage to which Baba and Gurumayi belong. By tapping
into this mother lode of grace, we can have meditations
and spiritual experiences that we could not have
dreamed possible.

For this is where the supreme adventure gets really exciting! Visions of Siddhas, of gods and goddesses, travel
to other realms, the experience of inner lights and music,
poetic inspiration, the destruction of harmful habits, the
removal of major psychological blocks, scriptural insights, the remembrance of past births, out-of-body experiences, the intoxication of divine love, and, finally, the
beatific vision of God himself: all these meditation experiences are possible for ordinary people like you and me
through the grace of a great being.

THE STAGES OF MEDITATION

The *Shiva Sutras* say, "The stages of yoga are filled
with fascinating wonders," and in the course of our inner

journey there are different realms and stages through which we will pass. Some of these stages are so amazing that we need the help of the scriptures and the Guru to understand them. For this reason I'd like to outline some of the main landmarks of this journey, as I've seen them, and as revealed by Baba and Gurumayi. I should say right at the outset that the definitive text on this inner journey is Swami Muktananda's spiritual autobiography, *Play of Consciousness. Play of Consciousness* is a kind of inner travel guide, a spiritual Baedeker. Any questions left unanswered here can be resolved by looking in its pages.

A MAP OF THE HEART

This body is a lotus which has four petals, the physical, the subtle, the causal, and the supracausal. Within each body there is another body. Many people complain about not having experiences in meditation because they only remain in the first petal, the physical body. Sometimes they go a little deeper, to the second petal, the subtle body, which corresponds to the dream state. This subtle body appears in meditation as a thumb-sized white light. The causal body, which corresponds to the state of deep sleep, is the size of a fingertip, and is dark. The supracausal body is a tiny, tiny blue dot or pearl. From this tiny blue pearl, which is the Self, everything springs forth. It is the seed of the universe, the seed of the heart.

In this statement, Gurumayi gives us a bird's-eye view of the inner landscape and a complete map of the spiritual journey. In meditation, we journey inward from the physical body and the state of waking consciousness to deeper petals of our being and subtler states of con-

sciousness until at last we enter into the blue dot, the
pearl of great price, and through this union become one
with our own true Self and the entire universe.

In Siddha meditation, this movement inward happens
quite naturally. Usually, the Shakti first works on the
outer petal, the physical body, strengthening and purifying it. As I have recounted, as soon as I sat and repeated
the mantra, my body would be seized by a superconscious power and I'd find myself assuming hatha yoga
postures that I had never done or even seen before. I did
shoulderstands, headstands, the fish, the bow, the locust,
and the plow pose, while different types of breathing exercises came to me spontaneously. These "meditations"
were so strenuous that I would finish them panting,
bathed in sweat. I had not worked out so hard since
wrestling in prep school. Afterward, I felt wonderful,
however—better than I had in years. I could feel the
prana surging in my body, my appetite became sharp and
regular, and at night I slept like a god.

This is the first task that meditation performs, to reju-
venate our physical body. For only when our body is
strong and healthy can we go beyond it to the inner Self.
Thus the Upanishads say: "The first signs of progress on
the path of yoga are health, a sense of physical lightness,
clearness of complexion, a beautiful voice, an agreeable
odor of person, and freedom from craving."[1]

KRIYAS

Later I learned that these yogic movements were
known as *kriyas*. Kriyas, in fact, may occur on many different levels of our being: mental and emotional as well
as physical. As the awakened Shakti unfolds throughout
our system, it begins to perform a general housecleaning,

removing those physical, mental, and emotional blocks that keep us feeling limited and small.

One of the first tasks it performs is to release us from addictions—smoking, drinking, drug taking, and overeating. As we discover a constant and independent source of bliss within, our need for outer intoxicants and stimulants falls away. The seeds of old habits are destroyed, and we begin to experience freedom from compulsive behavior, and a natural and authentic happiness.

This inner cleansing, however, is not always pleasant. We may experience intense sadness or anger, relive memories both trivial and traumatic, or feel pain or heat in different parts of our body. In the beginning, addictions may become stronger before they are removed. Sometimes as we meditate, the expanding Shakti encounters the germs of latent illnesses, and as they are expelled from our system we may suffer some symptoms. Gurumayi advises her students to consult a doctor if this occurs. Such symptoms are quite common, however.

Several months after I started to meditate, I began to have all the symptoms of intense dysentery. Despite the discomfort, I felt happy and strong; I just couldn't keep any food in my body. The moment I ate anything it exited the other end! My doctor, after ordering a full G.I. series, could find nothing wrong with me, and shortly thereafter the dysentery stopped of its own accord, never to return. Afterward, however, my entire digestive system felt quite restored.

But though these kriyas are occasionally unpleasant, we should remember they are entirely beneficial. Also, they are temporary. It is only the Shakti cleaning us out and making us new.

In fact, it is our general ignorance and our misconceptions about this great process of divinization that inspired Baba to first divulge the secrets of Siddha Yoga, wisdom which for millennia had been kept secret or veiled in metaphor. Though already an accomplished yogi when he received shaktipat, Baba knew almost nothing about the effects of the wakened kundalini and suffered intensely from his own wrong understanding of the kriyas that followed, thinking that he had somehow strayed from the path. It was only when he discovered a scripture[2] that explained the divine nature of shaktipat and the transforming process of Siddha Yoga that his fears vanished and he was able to resume his practices with joy. Having suffered from this ignorance himself, he revealed these secrets to spare us what he and others have undergone. He advises: "Think of everything you undergo, all the kriyas, as the blessings of the divine Goddess Chiti, Universal Consciousness, and offer them up to Her. If you do this, you will become calm and peaceful."[3]

There are some meditators who do not have any physical kriyas. This is because they do not need them. The Shakti is a superconscious power that shapes our sadhana according to our needs. In my own experience, as my body became purified, these physical movements lessened and then practically ceased. My meditations became deeper, stiller, and I began to see the white light that Gurumayi describes.

TANDRA

As we pass beyond the first petal, we enter into a marvelous state known as *tandra*. The scriptures also call it *yoganidra:* "yogic sleep." They call it this because the state of tandra is somewhat like the dream state, but because it is a state of meditation, everything we see in it is true. In this state we acquire a divine eye, unbounded by time and space, and we can see what is happening many miles or years away. We may have visions of the Guru or of other saints, see glimpses of our past lives, or experience extraordinary states of devotion or knowledge. We may even receive gifts, commands, medicine, or mantras from the Guru or other saints.

At one point in my sadhana I developed a persistent pain in my left foot. I went to my doctor, who said to me, "Mr. Hayes, you're getting old. These aches and pains come with age." "Old?" I said. "I'm thirty-five!" So I went to see an acupuncturist. He stuck pins in me for several months, but the pain did not go away. Then one morning in the tandra state of meditation, I saw a Catholic priest. I didn't know who he was, but I knew he was a Siddha. He handed me a bag of bay leaves and told me, "Make these into tea." He also showed me that the pain in my foot was a part of that same karmic affliction that had crippled me as a doctor in Liverpool, and had caused my foot to be slightly turned at birth.

When I came out of meditation I had some difficulty accepting what I had seen. Frankly, I was skeptical. I didn't see how ordinary bay leaves could cure anything, much less a sore foot. But I bought some anyway, and made them into tea. It had a mild, pleasant taste. I drank it twice a day. Within three days the pain in my foot had gone away, never to return.

I should add that everything we see in meditation may not be sublime. We may experience intense sexual feelings, or see ourselves engaged in actions which we long ago renounced. In some meditations I would see myself drinking alcohol, smoking, and eating meat. This is nothing to worry about. Baba says these are all welcome signs. It means the Shakti is doing its work very well. Past impressions from this and other lifetimes are being stirred up and flushed out by the awakened kundalini.

Sometimes, too, we may have experiences that are highly auspicious, but somewhat frightening. We may see fires burning, great conflagrations. We may see strange

beings; cobras or other snakes. But no matter what we
see, we should remember that in Siddha meditation we
are under the protection of the Siddha Guru, and nothing
can harm us.

LAYA YOGA

Siddha Yoga comprises the eight classical yogas, and
one of these eight is laya yoga, the yoga of inner sounds
and lights. Many, many people experience the meditation
energy in this way. The lights of the various bodies, described by Gurumayi, are all manifestations of laya yoga,
and by concentrating on them we can deepen our meditation. It's not a matter of *trying* to see them. Gurumayi
said one night in Mexico City: "Last night I talked about
the white light and somebody wanted to know if he
should be visualizing it. It is not a matter of visualizing
the white light. When the kundalini is awakened, there *is*
light, an inner explosion."[4]

The Upanishads explain: "In meditation, you may see
forms resembling snow, crystals, smoke, fire, lightning,
fireflies, the sun and moon. All these visions precede the
light of God."[5]

Certainly, the most amazing light of all is the blue dot,
or pearl. This is an electric-blue dot which may flash before your eyes, both in and out of meditation. It is the
light of the supracausal petal, the body of the Self, and
when you see it you should regard it as having seen God
himself. Sometimes it may appear to be black or brown,
but this is only because of impurities in our vision. As we
continue to meditate, its true nature will become known.
Baba says that as we meditate we begin to see this blue
dot more and more and for longer and longer periods of
time.

Accompanying this pearl is an amazing music. It is

called in the yogic tradition, *anahata nada,* or "unstruck sound." It is also known on other paths as the Name, the Word, the music of the spheres, or the choiring of angels.[6] This angelic music is always going on inside us. It is said to be "unstruck" because it isn't made by two things clashing together. It is the music of the space of Consciousness, the sweet reverberation of the Self; it is *Om,* the vibration of the blue pearl, the voice of kundalini.

This *nada* takes a thousand forms. We may hear it as different chants or mantras, as the sound of a bell, a horn, strings, flute, thunder, water, or electronic sounds. We may hear it in both the waking state and in meditation.

The form nada takes is not important. What is important is that when we hear it, we merge our mind with this inner sound. Gurumayi has spoken at length about this inner music. She has said that if we live our life according to its rhythms, we can never go wrong.

OUT OF THIS WORLD

The light of meditation is ever-new. As we continue to meditate, we may travel to other worlds. These other worlds are perfectly real. Many great sages have written about them, but it is difficult to believe in them unless you've had a direct experience. These worlds are not physical, but subtle. They are made of consciousness. For this reason we cannot visit them in our physical body. However, in meditation our soul can go there and return in a flash.

One of the worlds we can visit is *pitruloka,* the world of ancestors. Here the departed souls of righteous people live until their next incarnation. Once I saw my grandmother there, my Nana. She was sitting on a stone wall, saying her rosary, and taking care of a little boy. Though there was no sun, the light was good. The whole sky shone like mother-of-pearl. She seemed surprised to see me. But I quickly reassured her, "I'm not dead—meditating." We talked for a while. I noticed the small brown penny-shaped birthmark she had had on her left temple— a detail I had not thought about since she had died, more than fifteen years before. She gave me some advice. Then, suddenly, the world disappeared and I found myself in my apartment in New York City, coming up out of meditation.

This extraordinary experience, of course, was not of my doing. I was not trying to visit heaven. I was simply trying to meditate on my inner Self and to repeat the mantra *Om Namah Shivaya*. Nor can I explain to you the mechanics behind this astral journey. It happened according to the will of God and the extraordinary munificence of the Goddess Kundalini.

In addition to the world of departed souls, there are realms inhabited by Siddhas and many different types of celestial beings. Through the grace of the Guru, we may visit these, too.

THE GODS

One morning while I was meditating I went very deep within. Suddenly I heard the peal of giant bells and saw flares and sunbursts of white light. Then I looked up and saw a face staring down at me through the inner darkness. It was the face of a statue with wild archaic eyes, and it was luminous and bristling with Shakti and power. Then the face turned into an owl and an inner voice declared, "You have just seen Pallas Athena."

When I came out of meditation, my hair was standing on end and my whole body felt saturated with power. Before this, I had not believed in gods or goddesses. But now my whole attitude changed. The gods, I saw, were all inside me; the myths and legends all were true. It was I who had not understood their secret language.

Sitting on my magic carpet, I flew to other realms. There I heard the choiring of angels, the flute of Krishna, the pipes of Pan. There I saw Athena, protectress of heroes, and "heard old Triton blow his wreathed horn."[7]

FINAL REALIZATION

There are many, many more experiences that a meditator may have, but eventually, toward the culmination of our sadhana, we enter into the blue pearl. There we have what the scriptures call the realization of God with form. We see within the miraculous precincts of the blue pearl whatever form of God we worship. If we're Christian, we see Jesus; if Buddhist, Buddha. But even seeing this supreme Being, Baba tells us, is not the end of our journey:

Finally, as you meditate and meditate, one day the Blue Pearl will explode, and its light will fill the universe, and you will experience your all-pervasiveness. This experience is the culmination of sadhana, the ultimate realization. In this state, you merge into the body of God. It was after experiencing this that the great Shankaracharya proclaimed with firm conviction, "I am Shiva."[8]

Many paths make many claims, but Siddha Yoga makes the grandest claim of all. For it says that if we pursue our meditations faithfully, according to the commands of the Guru and with the love of God in our hearts, we will attain the final state of Siddhahood, of infinite bliss, of total and permanent oneness with the Self.

HOW TO MEDITATE

Classically, the scriptures say, the best time to meditate is between the hours of three A.M. and six A.M. However, when we are meditating by the power of Guru's grace we do not have to be overly concerned with conditions. In a way, whenever we begin to repeat the mantra, we are setting up an ideal meditative environment.

The question of place, however, is of greater importance. While a great being is always in the state of meditation, for those of us who are on the path, environment is crucial. Meditation, like sleep, needs to be courted, induced. And while you can probably sleep sitting up on a bus while the guy next to you listens to his radio, isn't it much easier to sleep in your own dark, quiet bedroom?

For this reason, make a special space for meditation. A separate room is ideal, but if that's not convenient, the unused corner of a room will do. This area should be used exclusively for spiritual practices. After a while the Shakti will build up there, making meditation come more easily. If you wish, you can make a small altar and place on it pictures of God or of the Guru. Burning incense and chanting where you meditate purifies the atmosphere and also enhances your meditation.

Sit in a chair, or on the floor. Wear loose, warm clothing and have a blanket or a shawl handy in case you get cold. Sit on a piece of wool. The purpose of this is to insulate the meditation energy from contact with the ground, keeping it inside us.

Get a timer. A simple kitchen timer or alarm clock will do. This way you will not have to worry about how long you are meditating. Set the timer for anywhere between twenty minutes and an hour.

Now get comfortable. If you're sitting on the floor, sit

cross-legged, or in the half-lotus. Fold your hands in your lap, or if you wish, you can touch the tips of your thumbs and index fingers together in the *chin mudra* and rest them on your knees. Keep your spine erect. Let your breath flow naturally. However, if in the course of meditation your breathing stops or changes, let it. If you hear noises outside, witness them, but do not become emotionally involved. Simply incorporate them into your meditation. Now close your eyes and let your mind go slack and still. Don't think; rest in that thought-free feeling. If you can't do that, then use one of the following techniques.

TURN WITHIN

Instead of meditating on something outside of you, which is what we do all day, turn your attention deep within. Close your eyes. Reverse the flow of your senses. Don't let your energy spill out into the world, but turn it inward toward its source. By focusing your attention within like this, great power is created—the way the rays of the sun when concentrated by a lens can start a fire.

MEDITATE ON THE SELF

Meditate on the Self, not on the thoughts of your mind. The Self is the one who watches your thoughts, the witness of your mind. Watch the watcher.

MEDITATE ON THE SELF AS THE SELF

Don't meditate on the Self as if it were a walnut, an object completely other than you. Meditate on the Self *as* the Self. You are the Self. Become the Self. For this moment, at least, stop identifying with your physical body, your mind, or your emotions. Be Shiva, the Self of all.

MEDITATE ON A GREAT BEING

Patanjali recommends that we meditate on a being who is "beyond attachment and aversion." Choose whatever form of God you love, or meditate on the form of the Guru, or on a saint. As you do, you will absorb that being's state and qualities.

MEDITATE ON
THE SPACE BETWEEN THE BREATHS

As the breath comes in, there is a moment when it stops—and dissolves inside—before the next expiration begins. Similarly, as the breath goes out, there is a moment where it stops—and merges on the outside—before the next inspiration occurs. Meditate on this space between the breaths. Place your mind in that thoughtless hollow, first on the inside, then on the outside. Where there is no breath there is no thought, and where there is no thought there is no mind; where there is no mind, the Self stands revealed. This space between the breaths is like a door in the mind, a secret panel that allows us to escape the room of our finite consciousness.

SEE THE THOUGHTS THAT ARISE AS A
PLAY OF CONSCIOUSNESS

Even if thoughts continue to arise in your mind, detach from them. See them all as Consciousness. Look at the *material* of your thoughts, rather than at their "meaning." Every thought, no matter how interesting or how unappealing, is only Consciousness in a different form, just as every wave is a part of the sea. Watch the waves of your thoughts arise and subside. From where do they arise? And what do they dissolve back into?

AFTER MEDITATION

It's not only our thoughts and emotions that are made of Consciousness. This whole world, the Siddhas tell us, is made of Consciousness as well. Even after you come out of meditation, hold the awareness that the world is the manifestation of God; see the earth as the body of the divine Shakti. See everything that happens to you, good or bad, as God's grace. Regard everyone you meet as the flame of God. The *Yoga Vasishtha* says, "The world is as you see it." When you see the world as Consciousness, it becomes Consciousness. When you regard yourself as Shiva, you yourself become the Lord.

CHAPTER 8

STUDY AND SERVICE: LIGHT ON THE PATH

Uddalaka: *"Have you asked for that knowledge by which we hear the unhearable, see the unseeable and know that which cannot be known?"*

Svetaketu: *"What is that knowledge, sir?"*

Uddalaka: *"Just as by knowing a single lump of clay, my son, all things that are made out of clay are known, the difference between them being only a matter of words . . . so is that knowledge, by knowing which we know all."*

—Chandogya Upanishad

The root of human misery is ignorance of our true nature. This root is called *anava mala,* that contraction which makes us think and feel "I am imperfect," "I am not Shiva."

From this root delusion springs a great tree with two main branches: *mayiya mala* and *karma mala.* The mayiya mala causes us to see differences in what is essentially a play of the one supreme Consciousness. Because of this we identify different things as good or bad, high or low, beneficial or harmful, spiritual or worldly. Under the influence of the karma mala we act, attempting to secure what is "good" and to avoid what is "bad." By these actions we accrue karma, becoming involved in the cycle of samsara, the endless round of birth and death. In this way the infinite eternal Being descends to earth and is crucified on the tree of Space and Time.

And yet, as should be apparent by now, all that is required to end our suffering is to destroy the root from which this tree of suffering springs. When its root is cut by the sword of knowledge, the whole fantastic edifice it supported withers and dies.

For this reason the Guru tells us, "You are Shiva. God dwells within you, as you." Upon hearing this only once the great ninth-century saint Shankaracharya was realized on the spot.

RIPENING

For most of us, however, this is not the case. Often, even after hearing the Truth, nothing really "happens." This is because knowing the Truth intellectually and actually realizing it are two different things. The seeker himself must ripen before he can eat the fruit in his hand.

Two of the best ways to bring about this ripening are through study and service. Through the first, we consolidate the knowledge we've gained in meditation, while through the second, we put it to the test.

Baba liked to tell of the yogi who lived alone in a forest cave. Believing he had attained the Absolute, he left the cave and went to the marketplace to give a sermon on universal love. As soon as he got there, he was jostled by someone; someone else stepped on his foot. "You idiots!" he cried. And that was that.

JNANA YOGA

Just as ignorance is at the root of suffering, so knowledge is at the root of liberation. Because of this, Siddha Yoga does not rely on blind faith. Gurumayi has said, "Knowledge without love is dry, but love without knowledge is madness!"

This right understanding is known as jnana yoga, the yoga of wisdom. In fact, Baba used to say that right understanding was even more important than inner experience; if you have right understanding, the experience is sure to follow, whereas if you have the experience without right understanding, it will be useless.

Just the other day, for instance, a Siddha Yoga student told me about the "demon" she had seen in meditation. She was quite upset. She described it to me in great detail —the swarthy skin, the coal-black eyes, the long, curled mustache. When she was finished I showed her a picture in a book on Indian art and statuary. She gasped: "That's it!" Then we read the caption. It wasn't a demon at all, but a celestial being!

Immediately she became ecstatic. She ran to her husband. She had seen a celestial being in meditation and it had blessed her! Of course she had every reason to be overjoyed. But what had changed? Not her experience. Only her understanding.

This is the purpose of this book, and of the dozens of books and thousands of talks by Baba and Gurumayi: to awaken us to a fresh appreciation of our own inner greatness and a renewed knowledge of who and what we really are. The difference between a great being and an ordinary person is not one of worth, but one of understanding. While both contain the Truth in its fullness, a great being knows it, while an ordinary person does not. For this reason the Siddha yogini Bahinabai says, "God exists in your own feelings."

BOOKS

"He who glows in the depths of your eyes—that is Brahman; that is the Self of yourself. He is the Beautiful One, he is the Luminous One. In all the worlds, forever and ever, he shines!"[1] In Siddha Yoga, the pure water of this divine perception wells up spontaneously from within. However, even so, it must be primed and clarified by contemplation and study. Gurumayi recounts:

I remember thinking one time that I did not have to read the scriptures or philosophies and I did not really have to listen to Baba's talks, either. Somehow, just by performing my daily actions, I thought, I would go across. When I was well-anchored in this kind of knowledge, Baba called me in one day. He always waited for the moment when you were totally anchored in your wrong understanding. He said, "Are you reading the Bhagavad Gita?"

I said, "No."

"What book are you reading these days?"

I looked at him and said, "Book?"

He said, "Yes, yes, you should be reading books. You think you are going to attain something without reading books?"

I was stunned because he had often said, "You don't need books to know God, you don't need books to know the truth, you don't need books to attain God-realization." And here he was saying I should read books. I gave him a blank look.

He said, "Go right now to the library and get ten books. You should take only one week to finish each one."[2]

THE SCRIPTURES

This is one of the things that most impresses me about Siddha Yoga: its profound respect for knowledge. Though Baba was a liberated being who had gone beyond all scriptures and social conventions, he continually demonstrated his respect for the scriptures by adhering to their injunctions. In fact he was joyously absorbed in rereading the *Vijnana Bhairava* during the final weeks of his life. Nor is Gurumayi any different in this respect. Everything she teaches has a sound scriptural basis, and even as I write, she is compiling a great spiritual library in South Fallsburg in order to preserve the spiritual heritage of the past.

Both of these masters afford the scriptures this place of honor, not out of some hidebound sense of tradition, but because they recognize them for what they are: the spiritual logs and diaries of great beings who have trod the inner path before them. In this way also, the scriptures can serve as a touchstone for our experience. When our own experiences agree with the scriptures and with our Guru's commands, we can be certain of their authenticity.

Conversely, beware of any so-called teacher who claims he or she has discovered a "new" path, or who recommends practices not recognized by the scriptures. The very nature of the Truth is that it is eternal and unchanging. If a "new" truth comes along one day, how true can it really be?

INTERPRETATION

When studying the scriptures, however, there are a few things to keep in mind. The first is that you must read them with some intelligence and sophistication. A literal, fundamentalist approach is not always correct. There is a verse in the *Bhagavad Gita* that says, "What is day for a yogi is night for a worldly person, and what is day for a worldly person is night for a yogi." I knew a fellow who interpreted this verse to mean that he should sleep all day and stay up all night!

On the other hand, there are parts of the scriptures that *are* meant to be taken literally. As we've seen, travel to other realms and the vision of gods and celestial beings are more than religious archetypes and literary metaphors. So how, then, does one study and interpret the scriptures with correct understanding?

Once again, it helps to have the guidance of a teacher. For while the Truth doesn't change, different times and individuals demand its different applications. "What has become outmoded or mere empty ritual should not be imposed on a new generation."[3] For example, certain yogic scriptures praise the practice of long fasts and harsh austerities, but as Baba pointed out, these scriptures were written during the *Krita Yuga,* an earlier age when people had more physical strength, while in this age, the *Kali Yuga,* the same results can be achieved through meditation and chanting.

But even more important, the Guru can give us an inner experience of That of which the scriptures speak. Baba says, "What is understood intellectually through books and study can be experienced directly through Siddha Yoga."[4] Once we've had that experience, the scriptures come alive and we can see the Truth behind the words and traditions of every path.

STUDY

It is for this reason that study is important. Study refines the mind, which is both the means and obstacle to liberation. As we contemplate spiritual truths, these truths begin to percolate through our consciousness and to color our perceptions, leading us eventually to a new experience of the world and of ourselves. This experience is essentially one of Self-recognition, of rediscovering who and what we really are. Gurumayi says, in finishing her story:

When Baba asked me to read those books, I really had no idea what I would gain by reading them. It was not

until I read them that I had the experience of the yoga
of wisdom. Lord Krishna says:

> "Endowed with wisdom, a person casts off
>   in this life
>   both good and evil deeds.
> Therefore devote yourself to yoga.
> Yoga is skill in action."[5]

SEVA

In the above verse from the *Bhagavad Gita,* action and
wisdom elide. We cannot perform actions without knowledge, and we cannot test our knowledge until we act
upon it.

One of the best ways to test and broaden our understanding is through the practice of *Guruseva,* selfless service to the Guru. *Seva* is an ancient and time-honored
practice. It is also a very mysterious one.

Once a seeker went to a Guru and asked for his teaching. The Guru said, "My teaching is this: Thou art That,"
but the seeker couldn't understand him. So the seeker
went to another Guru, who agreed to teach him under
one condition: the seeker would first have to serve him
for twelve years. The seeker agreed and was given the
task of picking up cow dung. When the twelve years were
up he went back to the Guru. The Guru told him: "My
teaching is this: Thou art That." And at that moment the
seeker was enlightened.

What had changed? Not the Truth. It was the very
same teaching that the first Guru had given him twelve
years earlier, only now the seeker was ready to receive
it. This is seva's main task: to purify our inner being so
that we may be able to fully imbibe the teachings. The
broom we pick up to clean the ashram walk ends up
sweeping our heart as well. Seva removes blocks, blocks

in our heart, blocks in our head, blocks in our under-standing.

Nor should we delude ourselves in thinking that the Guru *needs* us to do seva. While it may appear on the surface that the service we perform helps the Guru, it is really the other way around. It is the seeker, not the Guru, who benefits through seva.

The fact is, Guruseva is a great means to liberation and a precious spiritual gift. Gurumayi has said that we get the opportunity to do seva only when the accumulated merits of many lifetimes ripen and bear fruit. Jnaneshwar says:

> *If you have acquired the worth by means of which you can serve the Guru, you should consider yourself to be extremely fortunate, to be extremely blessed. You don't get that desire to serve the Guru without God's grace.*

To give you some idea of how seva works, I'd like to share with you my own experience of some seva I did recently.

In May of 1986, during Gurumayi's first world tour, I was asked to serve as master of ceremonies at her evening programs at the Manhattan Center in New York. Basically, my job was to stand up and welcome the thousands of people who came nightly to see her, give a short talk on some aspect of yoga, and introduce the speakers and Gurumayi. However, first I was asked to attend a workshop on public speaking.

Frankly I was resistant to the whole idea of the workshop. I felt I had already come a long way since the first time I had introduced Gurumayi in New Orleans. That first night I had emceed I was absolutely terrified. As I gazed out on the crowd of several thousand people, my whole body was shaking. To compensate, I had written out every word I had to say, put my head down, and read from my notes.

The next morning, Gurumayi called for me. She said, "How long have you been studying yoga?" I said, "Seven years, Gurumayi." "Then why do you have to read from notes? Don't use notes. Just speak to the people. Speak to them from your experience, speak to them from your heart."

This seemed like good advice. So I reduced my notes to a single three-by-five notecard with key words on it. Since I wasn't reading anymore, I began to look up and out at the audience as I spoke. And I realized then how my strength was my weakness, how all my life I had used literature both as a means to communicate with people and as a way to keep them at arm's length. In short order, Gurumayi had torn down this wall.

And so, a year later, when someone stood up and said, "This workshop is going to transform your life," I remember thinking, "That's ridiculous." It wasn't that I didn't believe in transformation. It was simply that, after seven years of Siddha Yoga, every part of life had already been completely transformed.

At the end of the workshop we videotaped our talks. I was pleased with the way mine had gone. I thought I had done a pretty good job. Thus I was appalled when I actually got to see myself on the television monitor. I scarcely recognized the person. A dry, bespectacled intellectual was droning on and on about Siddha Yoga in this deadly boring tone.

And the funny thing was that I didn't *feel* that way inside. Inside, I felt light, playful, and full of love. And yet watching myself on television, I would never have known it—for, I realized now, *I wasn't letting my love show.*

This insight swung open some huge inner door for me. I began to see how all my life I had hidden my love for fear that it would be laughed at or rejected. And as I contemplated this insight I saw how I was not alone. All of us have so much love inside us, but for one reason or another we don't let it show!

In the following weeks while I emceed the programs in Manhattan, Love became my constant meditation. Gurumayi had always talked about divine love, but I had subtly tuned out whenever the subject arose, tuning back in when she returned to the subjects of philosophy and inner experience. And I felt now, through the magic of seva, that my ears had been unplugged and I was really hearing her for the first time.

Now when I welcomed people to the evening programs, I tried to speak to them from that place of love. They say spiritual growth is about raising your consciousness, but I felt as if mine were dropping—from my head down to my heart! And as it did, I felt my stiffness dissolve, for it seemed the more I revealed my love to other people, the more I felt it inside myself.

Stranger still, people started treating me very differently. Instead of asking me intellectual questions about Vedanta or Kashmir Shaivism, they began showering me with affection.

This made me distinctly uncomfortable, at first. And I began to see that I had difficulty not only expressing affection, but receiving it as well. Love was not for macho men like me. Love was, well . . . for girls.

And yet another part of me knew that this transformation was absolutely vital to my well-being. And besides, it was ecstatic. My heart was opening, and with it the flow of an incredible elixir.

SKILL IN ACTION

But there were other lessons besides love that I got from this one seva. The scriptures say, *Shivena shiva sadhana:* "Do the sadhana of Shiva by becoming Shiva." I had never understood exactly how this was to be done. And then one night, as I was doing my seva, I realized that *Shiva was my very best self.*

Kierkegaard tells a story of an ugly, evil king who falls in love with a beautiful and virtuous maiden. Since he knows such a girl will never marry a man like him, he approaches a witch, who makes him the mask of a wise and noble prince. Donning the mask, he woos and marries the princess and, playing the part of a good and noble king, reigns happily with his queen for many years.

Then one night the witch appears in the king's court, demanding as payment for her services the firstborn child of the couple's union. The king, horrified, tells her to get out. Enraged, the sorceress threatens to expose the king —and reaching up, she removes his mask. But miraculously, over the years, the king's face has changed, becoming identical to the noble mask.

This fair and noble prince is Shiva. And Shiva was what emceeing for Gurumayi was forcing me to be. I had to look my best, act my best, be my best. When people were upset, I had to be calm. When there were questions, I had to know the answers. I was the *master* of ceremonies. Everyone else could fall apart, but I had to be strong and warm and sharp and kind and clear. There was no room for self-consciousness, hesitations, or doubts. For those few hours at least, I had to put away all my human foibles and practice being princely and divine.

And all the time, there were constant tests to keep me on my toes and see what I had really attained. On the one hand, I had to make sure the program went according to schedule; on the other hand, the schedule was subject to change at any time. One night, as I stood up to welcome the audience, I was handed a note that read: "The speaker's late. Give an extemporaneous twenty-minute talk on chanting."

Another night I had a talk all prepared when the speaker before me spoke on the same subject. When I stood up to follow him, something inside me told me not to go ahead, but since I'd already prepared the talk, I went ahead with it anyway.

I hadn't said more than a couple of sentences, however, before the microphone went dead. I looked around; the lights were still on. It didn't seem to be a power failure. I checked the switch on the mike to see if I had flicked it off by accident. No, the switch was on. "Hello," I said. "Hello, hello." Nothing. And then, from within, I knew what had happened. Gurumayi had turned off the sound on me.

If you ever want to have an experience of the Self, stand up in front of an audience of two thousand people with a dead mike, knowing your Guru doesn't want to hear what you're saying. Your brain freezes and your mind stops.

But what amazed me most was that I realized Gurumayi would do almost *anything* to make me grow— even if it came to disrupting her own program. And in that moment my discomfort vanished, and I was thrilled. For she had given me what I had come to her for; she was my teacher and she had taught me a lesson in such a way that I was not likely to forget it.

And the lesson she had taught me was this: Trust yourself. Trust your own inner feelings. Listen to your heart, not to your mind. Follow the schedule of your life but listen to the inner music and be prepared for change at any time.

Later that night I talked to a swami who had done the same emcee seva. He told me Gurumayi would often call him up on the phone next to the podium just before the program was to begin, and proceed to rearrange the entire schedule.

One night, the swami, who was a meticulous soul, couldn't take it anymore. He burst out, "Gurumayi, this is driving me crazy. The whole program is planned so carefully . . . and then you change it. Why?"

There was a pause; then Gurumayi said, "Oh, *Swamiji*, don't you know I create these crises on purpose, so that when a real crisis comes up in your life, you'll be able to handle it with grace?"

This is how a great being teaches—not just through words and lectures, but by thrusting us into situations where we are forced to grow. Service to such a being teaches us grace under pressure and skill in action. When performed for a true Guru, seva becomes an instrument through which the ethereal maxims of the scriptures enter into the flesh and blood of our life. It is not unlikely that what I learned about love and what my friend the swami learned about poise was something we would have arrived at after years in therapy. But in my case it had all happened in three weeks! In the hothouse environment of seva, inner growth is forced and spiritual truths bloom with an astonishing rapidity and power. Nor is my story unique. Anyone who has served a great being could tell you many similar tales.

Furthermore, the lessons which we learn through seva spill over into our mundane life. The love that opened up inside me during those weeks in Manhattan did not go away when Gurumayi left and the programs ended.

In fact, the excellence of all these spiritual practices—chanting, meditation, study, and service—is that they transform our life from the inside out. This is the bottom line. Our delusions are removed, our fears and limitations fall away, and our true nature begins to shine. The nature of this transformation is paradoxical, however, for as the Siddhas tell us, we become who we've been all along. In the end, all our searching only leads us home. Or as T. S. Eliot says,

> *And the end of all our exploring*
> *Will be to arrive where we started*
> *And know the place for the first time.*[6]

CHAPTER 9

SATSANG: THE COMPANY
OF THE TRUTH

It was like a stream
running into the dry bed
of a lake.
Like rain
pouring on plants
parched to sticks.
It was like
this world's pleasure
and the path to liberation
both walking toward me.
Seeing the face of the Master,
O Lord,
I was made worthwhile.

—Akkamahadevi

When all is said and done, Siddha Yoga is the path of love. Not every student can serve the Guru directly; not everyone may chant for hours or have visions in meditation, but everyone must experience love within their hearts. Without this love—this bond between the Guru and the disciple—the miracles of Siddha Yoga do not arise.

This love creates in the disciple an irresistible longing to make contact with the Guru. This contact is the sweetest and most edifying thing in the world. The sage Narada, in his *Bhakti Sutras,* writes: "The primary means of receiving divine love is through the grace of a *mahapurusha,* a great being. Contact with such a soul is rare and difficult to obtain, and yet, once obtained, unfailing in its effect. It comes about through God's grace."[1]

What constitutes such contact? Contact with a true Guru is not only experiencing his or her physical presence or touch. It is much subtler than that. For me it took the form of that book I bought, *Play of Consciousness,* one October morning in an uptown bookstore. Other people first make contact with the Guru through her picture or through her devotees. Some people first see her in dreams or in visions, even before they meet her in the waking state.

In the end, however, once this initial contact is made, the desire arises to be with the Guru in person. It is also the Guru's delight to be with her disciples.

SATSANG

To spend time in the company of a great being is known as satsang, "keeping the company of the Truth." Satsang is a spiritual practice that is available to all. Some people meet the Guru only once in their life; others come once a year, or on holidays, or when they feel a need to re-connect with their inner Self. Others, like myself, find the first meeting so intoxicating that we return again and again. The frequency with which we visit the Guru is up to us. The scriptures say that great beings are like deep pools and verdant trees in the desert of existence. They are there for everyone: the rich and the poor, the learned and the ignorant, the good and the bad—all have the right to bathe in their waters and to take refuge in their shade.

For this reason Siddha Yoga has no official membership. There are no dues to pay or vows to take. There are no degrees or credentials you must have or anything you must believe in. Nor should you ever think that you are too young or too old, too sinful or unworthy, to receive grace. Gurumayi has said: "Grace is love and love can be received by anyone, no matter who or how you are."

THE BENEFITS OF SATSANG

We seek out the company of the Truth for the very same reason that we keep anyone's company—for what we derive from it. Satsang takes advantage of a basic psychological principle that says: What we meditate upon, that we become. If we keep the company of thieves, it's not unlikely we'll become thieves. Similarly, if we keep the company of those in whom the Truth is shining, we eventually *become* that Truth.

How this transformation takes place is most mysterious. Baba said: "If you sit next to a physicist, you won't learn physics. If you sit next to a chef, you won't learn how to cook, but if you sit down next to a kundalini yogi, you will have an experience of the Truth."

In fact we may have this experience whether we want it or not! Once I overheard someone tell Gurumayi, "I wasn't really interested in meeting a Guru. I just came to see you because my friend wanted me to. And yet, the moment I walked into the room, I felt this incredible awakening." This happens because such a being as Gurumayi is anchored in the Self, and the Self is not a cold, inert principle, but a roaring, sparking blaze. "Such a yogi," the scriptures say, "gladdens the world with his moonlike rays." The *Shiva Sutras* say, *Danam atmajnanam:* "Knowledge of the Self is the gift that such a yogi gives to all."

And while this gift is supernatural, in other ways it's the most natural thing in the world.

A poet writes:

> *As a man feels desire when embracing a woman,*
> *Or fear when attacked by a ravenous beast,*
> *Or hot when standing in front of a fire,*

Or alone in a wild and wilderness place,
So very naturally in the company of a Siddha,
A person experiences great ecstasy and peace.[2]

This is the wonder of satsang. Of all the various spiritual techniques, it's the easiest, for there's nothing to do. It's like getting a tan. All you have to do is expose yourself to the sunlight. Nor is it that a Siddha has to focus personally upon each person, any more than that the sun has to concern itself personally with giving each individual a tan. For example, even though Bhagawan Nityananda rarely spoke, those who went to him found in his presence that their questions were often answered from within.

Because of this, it is not necessary to interact socially with the Guru. To come into her presence is enough. In the three years I knew Baba, he spoke to me exactly twice. Still, he transformed my life and gave me everything I ever needed.

Sometimes, of course, the Guru may give us individual instruction. The first time a friend of mine met Baba, he grabbed her hand and asked her, playfully, "Are you happy?" She wasn't at the time, but as she told me later, "He was such a nice old man that I didn't want to hurt his feelings, so I said, 'Yes, Baba,' and took my seat." The moment she sat down, however, she felt something open up inside her and wave after wave of bliss began to roll and rise up, splashing her heart. She looked at him, amazed. Nice old man, indeed! And she realized then that he had given her the *experience* of that happiness which, before keeping his company, she had only briefly glimpsed.

As for Gurumayi, my overwhelming experience while in her presence is the experience of love. Sometimes I sit for hours, watching her greet the thousands of people who come to see her, answering their questions, listening to their troubles, looking at snapshots of their loved ones, touching their babies, giving them her blessings.

The other day when I was with her, a group of seven very old American Indian women and one tiny little Indian girl embraced her gravely and with great dignity, one by one, then walked off in single file, their faces shining. Afterward one of the women told me, "When we were young we were told that before we died we must meet the Great White Buffalo Calf Woman. We are happy because we have met her today."

This is the wondrous thing about the Guru. Her inner being is so clean and lustrous that she is like a mirror in which we can see the face of our own Self. A Catholic nun confessed to me that after meeting Gurumayi she had begun to have the inner experience of Jesus. A lady from Delhi said that while meditating with Gurumayi she had seen Krishna dancing with the Gopis. In this way, the Guru is the perfect mirror.

THE WISH-FULFILLING TREE

The scriptures liken a great being to a wish-fulfilling tree. They say that whatever rightful desires we approach her with will be fulfilled. This, however, can be a two-edged sword. People used to ask Baba why he had received Self-realization from his Guru, Bhagawan Nityananda, when they had *also* gone to him and had not yet become realized. Baba used to say, "I received liberation because that's what I wanted. Other people came to my Guru wanting jobs, money, a husband, or children. And that's precisely what they got."

This is why it is important to approach such a being with a pure heart and pure desires. When such a one can grant your wishes, why ask for anything but the highest— for love of God and knowledge of the Self?

There was once a king whose life was saved by a peasant. He asked the peasant what he wanted for his reward. The peasant, who had just run out of slake lime to mix with his betel nut, asked the king for a pinch of lime. The king complied. When the peasant left, he turned to his prime minister in amazement and said, "I would have given that man a whole slake-lime mine. He could have had groves of betel nut. He could have had my *kingdom* if he had only said he wanted it, but instead, he asked for a pinch of dust!"

PRASAD

Sometimes a saint may distribute food or gifts. This is called *prasad,* and it is a traditional way that a saint gives us his or her blessing. The scriptures say: "Prasad destroys all misfortunes." If you receive such prasad, you should consider yourself extremely fortunate and understand it for what it is: the Guru's grace in the form of a gift.

Of course, the greatest prasad we can receive from the Guru is shaktipat, since this one gift contains all things. Just as within a tiny seed a whole banyan tree is enfolded, so the seed of grace the Guru implants in the disciple through shaktipat initiation eventually blossoms into the highest state of consciousness and bears the sweetest fruit.

INITIATION

In the olden days, shaktipat was given by a Guru to a few hand-picked disciples, and only after testing the disciples for many, many years. But Swami Muktananda, at the command of his Guru, changed all this. Through his compassion, he made the miracle of kundalini awakening available to all. Gurumayi has followed in his footsteps, holding regular programs, called Intensives, where shaktipat is given.

Traditionally, the Guru gives shaktipat in any one of four ways—through her touch, look, word, or thought. In Siddha Yoga, all these means may be employed.

First of all, the Guru can *will* that you receive shaktipat. This is called shaktipat by *sankalpa,* or thought. In this case, the Guru's physical presence is not even required. A Siddha Guru, by simply thinking about it, can awaken the kundalini of a person anywhere in the world. Thus Gurumayi, from her ashram in India, can give shaktipat to a group of students in, say, Milwaukee.

Touch is the second classic means of giving shaktipat. During some Intensives, while everyone meditates, Gurumayi moves through the meditation hall, touching people with her hand or with a wand of peacock feathers. Once, at an Intensive in New Orleans, Gurumayi touched the back of my spine. I felt the Shakti move along my backbone, then I was plunged immediately into a state of deep meditation in which I saw brilliant inner lights and heard the strange, sweet notes of a divine harmonica.

Such wonders happen because the Guru is a vast storehouse of Shakti, and just by contact with her, our own inner light is kindled. In fact, even "accidental" contact with such a great being may result in this awakening, as was the case for Kabir.

The third classic means of shaktipat initiation is through the Guru's word. The Guru's word generally means the mantra, by which we may come to know our own true Self.

Finally, there is shaktipat by look. Just by her looking at you (or you at her), a Siddha can awaken you. Baba's Guru, Bhagawan Nityananda, gave Baba shaktipat in this way. In fact, you may even receive shaktipat just by looking at photographs of Baba, or Gurumayi. Many thousands of people can attest to this phenomenon.

Other people receive initiation in a dream, at an evening program, or even by coming into contact with something the Guru has touched.

GOOD COMPANY

The purpose of yoga is transformation, and this transformation comes about through contemplation of the supreme Reality. For this, spending time with other seekers is essential, for just as business people discuss business, and artists art, so, in the company of saints and their devotees, the mind and thoughts very naturally focus on the Truth.

Good company is more than just other people, however. The food we eat, our personal habits, and the thoughts we hold in the mind are just as important as the people with whom we associate, and are an essential ingredient of spiritual practice.

Nor is it necessary to be in the constant physical presence of the Guru. In Siddha Yoga we meditate on our own Self. And while it is true the scriptures stress "surrender to the Guru," we should examine with intelligence what this "surrender to the Guru" really means. Baba says: "It does not mean having to stay very close to him or having to give him all your money or having to leave your family and your job and follow him wherever he goes. Nor does it mean becoming small and wretched, expecting someone to take care of you. To give yourself to the Guru means to constantly try to imbibe the Guru's instructions. . . . The Guru will never give you a command to make use of you for his own purposes. The Guru will give you a command only to transform your life. . . . This is the mystery of discipleship. All attainments come from the

Guru. . . . By surrendering to the Guru, you yourself become the Guru."[3]

SURRENDER TO THE GURU

This is the secret of Siddha Yoga—surrender to the Guru. Without this surrender we will never attain what this path has to offer. What we surrender is our ego, that part of ourselves that keeps us limited and small. It is like a raindrop merging into the ocean, or a seed surrendering itself to the soil. When the drop merges, it becomes the ocean; when the seed surrenders, it becomes a tree. Seeds that don't surrender their "seedness" only wither up and blow away. In the same way, all that we lose through surrender is our smallness and our limitations. And yet this surrender can be absolutely terrifying, for the ego resists it with all its wiles and might. For me, it has been both the crux and the hardest part of my sadhana, or spiritual life. And yet the mystics of all the great traditions declare this: that we must surrender our life to that divine force which flows through the master.

The greatness of having a living Guru is that this game of surrender takes on new force and meaning. It's easy to to say you've surrendered your life to God as you go about your usual business. But the Guru constantly tests our surrender to see if it's for real.

Once someone asked Kabir about surrender. Kabir was a weaver, and for the longest time he did not answer but went on about his weaving. At one point he dropped his shuttle. Though it was broad daylight, he asked a disciple to light a lantern so that he could search for it. The man did so, and picking up the shuttle, Kabir continued with his weaving. The questioner, thinking that Kabir had not heard him, repeated the question. Again Kabir said nothing. After a while he turned to his disciple and told him,

"Give this man some halvah. And be sure to put plenty of salt in it." The disciple did as he was ordered, and though salt had been added, the man was astonished to find that the halvah was very sweet. Once again he asked Kabir: "O Kabir, why won't you answer my question?"

Kabir said, "I've answered it twice. Why didn't you listen to my answer? I dropped my shuttle and told this fellow to light a lamp so I could find it. It is noon. What do I need with a lantern? And yet he did not say to me, 'O Kabir, what's wrong with you? Have you lost your reason?' Then I asked him to give you halvah and to put some salt in it. Everyone knows one puts sugar in halvah, not salt. And yet he did not say to me, 'O Kabir, you're getting old. You don't know what you're saying to me.' He did what I asked him to do. This is surrender to the Guru."

Do not think that this is just some story from the olden days, either. The same tests that were given then by the great beings are given here now; what was vital a thousand years ago is just as necessary today.

Once I was awakened in New York City at three in the morning by a phone call telling me that Gurumayi wanted me to take the next plane to Hawaii. There was one leaving from La Guardia, I was told, in an hour and a half. I was, of course, half asleep and I had work and appointments scheduled for the next day and the week ahead, but I said yes, packed a bag, and left right away. I had no idea how long I would be gone or even why I was going. And yet I knew that if I followed the Guru's command, everything would work out—somehow. When I got to Hawaii and called my secretary, she said my clients themselves had called that morning and canceled all their appointments for the week. I said aloha, and spent a blissful ten days doing some seva for Gurumayi.

In fact, never have I lost anything by doing the Guru's bidding. And if I've suffered, it's only been due to my own ego and resistance. Once Gurumayi told me to write something that I didn't believe to be true. Instead of surrendering to her greater wisdom and just doing it, I had all sorts of conniptions. I worked myself up into a veritable lather about my "journalistic integrity"—though in the end I wrote it anyway. Two years later, when the piece was finally published, what I had written *had come true* in the ensuing years. *My* way would have been untrue—though I was perfectly convinced I was right at the time.

Surrender, then, is an opening of the heart, a willingness to let the higher wisdom of divine love into our life. It's giving the ego a backseat, putting it at the service of a higher power. In this act of surrender everything is conjoined: faith and love, inner growth and self-denial. Jesus says, "Behold I stand at the door and knock. If any man hear me and open it he will sup with me and I with him." The Guru principle is always standing at our inner door, waiting. It has been standing there for all eternity. Surrender is this: that we listen to its knocking, open the door, and invite it in.

THE HUMAN HEART

Once a boy left home for Mecca to search for God. On his way he met a great dervish, who asked him where he was going. The child explained. The dervish then said, "It's a long way to Mecca, little boy. I tell you what— walk around me three times." The child did so, and immediately felt the presence of God within his heart. Then the dervish said, "Listen to what I tell you. Since Mecca was first built, God has never lived there. Since the human heart was created, God has never left it. Now you may go home."

If God really lived in mosques and temples, then we

wouldn't need the company of the lovers of the Truth. But as Kabir says, "I looked in both the mosque and temple. They were empty." The true church is the human body, and the great cathedral is the heart of a saint.

For this reason, the Siddhas say, we should keep the company of great beings and their devotees. Or as Baba has said: "There may be many great practices for attaining God, but satsang is the most sublime. Through satsang, one's desires are fulfilled, one learns to meditate ceaselessly on the supreme Self, and then one does not have to do any other kind of practice. When your faith in satsang increases, liberation will come looking for you."

A scripture puts it simply and quaintly: "Coming to know of a perfect being who has attained the Truth—become his friend."

CHAPTER 10

SIDDHA YOGA
IN THE WORLD:
VICTORY AND RETURN

*The joy of the world
is the bliss of samadhi.*

—Shiva Sutras

During the time I was writing this book, I lived a very happy, very disciplined life. I'd rise every morning at four o'clock, wash my hands and face, light a candle, then sit down in a corner of my bedroom and meditate on the Self. My apartment was small; it wasn't a fashionable address. But oh, what visions I had in it! I saw gods, goddesses! I traveled to other realms! Sometimes I heard intoxicating inner music or saw brilliant holy lights.

After meditation I'd lie down for a couple of minutes, and in that twilit interlude I had dreams in which I sometimes saw Baba, Gurumayi, or other Siddhas.

At six I'd get back up, eat a buttered bun, and drink some coffee. Then I'd dress and go outside.

The bus ride was always pleasant. The traffic was light, the pigeons heavy. I'd get off the bus at Eighty-sixth Street and Broadway, go to the ashram, and chant the *Guru Gita.* At the end we'd sing the ecstatic kirtan *Shri Krishna Govinda Hare Murare,* and with the harmonium and drum, the incense and candles, and the sun coming up outside on the city streets, I felt as if a vial of some precious oil were spilling out inside me.

When the chant was over, I'd jog the three miles home through Riverside Park, running for the better part of the way right along the river. I'd circle Grant's Tomb, then head for my apartment, sprinting up the seven flights of stairs. I'd take a shower, change my clothes, and be ready to work by 9:15.

Though the day had just begun, I had already put in three and a half hours of chanting, exercise, and meditation, and my body would be absolutely humming with prana, while my mind would feel serene and calm. Then I'd gather up my notebooks and pens and walk several blocks to the Cathedral Church of St. John the Divine. In good weather I'd sit in the sun on a stone bench in the Biblical Garden. There were some tame peacocks there whom I named Shiva and Shakti, and sometimes they would dance for me, fanning their tails.

When it was chill or rainy I'd go across Amsterdam Avenue to the Hungarian Pastry Shop. I'd eat a croissant with honey, washed down with café au lait, then open my notebook and get to work.

In those days I was also working on a novel called *A Bed in Hell,* and its writing amazed me. Though I had always been a slow, careful writer, the words came spilling out of me faster than I could write them down. It was as though I were eavesdropping on a conversation that was going on inside me, and even when I made revisions, it was less like rewriting than like listening again to the conversation to make certain I had transcribed it correctly.

And yet the things the characters were saying appalled me. I had wanted to write a "spiritual" novel, but my characters were not cooperating; they were not being very spiritual at all! Doctors and prostitutes, dictators and South American revolutionaries, torturers and heroes, thugs and saints, all began to dance in an enormous adventure. Some mornings I'd sit with my generals as we plotted the overthrow of their beloved country. Ah, the passionate speeches, the lightning bolts that flashed inside me, the martial ardors that stirred my blood! I wrote stuff I never knew. I wrote a whole chapter on guerrilla warfare, though I'd never been to war in this life. Finally I got scared. I thought, This can't be right; I must be making this up. So I bought the *Art of War* by Sun Tzu, the classic text on irregular warfare written in China about 400 B.C. And when I'd finished it I felt even more scared, because everything I'd written was perfectly correct. And yet I kept wondering, Why was I writing about outer war when what I was feeling was a tremendous inner peace?

So I wrote to Baba, telling him what was happening. He wrote me back at once: "After a person receives shaktipat, his whole life becomes yoga. It's not that writing is something separate. It's okay, the Shakti is doing its work very well. The Shakti is making use of your writing to broaden your understanding and deepen your experience."

In a flash, these words of the master revolutionized my understanding. For I saw now that I'd been making an artificial distinction between what was spiritual and what was mundane.

MOTHER EARTH

One of the great archaeological adventure stories of modern times was written by the British archaeologist Michael Dames, as described in his books *The Avebury Cycle* and *The Silbury Treasure*.

Dames had been fascinated by the neolithic dolmens and mounds with which the British Isles are studded— the circle at Stonehenge being the greatest and best-known. For years, he investigated the various mounds, attempting to fathom their meaning. Then one day, in a leap of vision, he saw that all the mounds and circles of stones throughout one whole area of England were not separate, but were related to each other. When connected by lines—the way children play "connect the dots"—they formed an immense figure of the Divine Mother, a landscape sculpture more than ten miles long. The Goddess's breasts, back, womb, and arms can all be seen in the landscape, and are still remembered in the place-names. To these ancient people, the Earth was literally the body of God.

With the spread of Christianity throughout Europe, this druidical vision was suppressed. In the East, however, it remained intact and has been an essential part of the vision of yoga.[1] To the Siddhas, Mother Earth is a living reality. Or as Baba puts it, "The Lord of the universe has become the universe."

According to this vision, everything is divine and everything, therefore, is capable of bringing us closer to the Self. Seated in this outlook, the Siddhas teach that our life on earth, our job, our duties, and our family are not an obstacle but a means to attaining God.

THEORY OF AESTHETICS

But how does one do this, how does one use the world to go beyond it? Soon after receiving Baba's letter, I came across a theory of aesthetics composed by the Siddha Abhinavagupta, of Kashmir.[2] This millennium-old scripture confirmed what Baba himself had written me, while explaining in more detail how the mundane and ordinary lead to the sublime. According to Abhinavagupta, a work of art is composed of different *rasas*—flavors, tastes— blended in a sublime and skillful way. Abhinavagupta identified eight main flavors. They are the erotic, the comic, the heroic, the marvelous, the odious, the terrible, the furious, and the pathetic. A work of art that has only one or two of these flavors is ultimately cloying, like a comic strip, or food that is only salty or sweet. Good food, like great art, is a blend of many subtle flavors. However, for a work of art to be truly successful, all its flavors must merge in the final rasa, called *shantarasa,* the taste of peace.

This is that *ahh!* we experience, that shock of recognition, that moment of exalted blissful stillness when a work of art has done its work. James Joyce, in *A Portrait of the Artist as a Young Man,* identifies it as that moment when "the mind is arrested and raised above desire and loathing."[3] What is especially interesting about Joyce's definition of art is that it is a combination of two of Patanjali's most famous sutras: "Yoga is the stilling of the thought-waves of the mind," and "Meditate on a being who is beyond attachment and aversion."[4]

This state of mental stillness, without attachment (desire) or aversion (loathing), is the end at which all great art and all true yoga aims. It is the same state for Easterners and Westerners, a place of mental equipoise and balance, of love and detachment. Or, as Abhinavagupta puts it: "To respond deeply to literature and to understand one's own Self are the same thing."

OUR LIFE AS ART

As in art, the spiritual path is not about creating a life that is bland, without any spice or variety of flavors. After we begin to meditate it's not that everyone begins to speak to us in soft respectful tones or that we walk around in flowing robes. What happens is that we begin to draw from the various elements of our life—even the odious and the terrible—that sweetness, that rasa, that taste of peace. Without this peace at the heart of our experience, all the other tastes and flavors of our life never lead to satisfaction.

DHARMA

No one, therefore, in the name of spirituality, need abandon his or her worldly duties in order to find the Self. In fact, the Siddhas insist that we must carry out our worldly responsibilities with zest, zeal, courage, and skill. Few of the saints of the Siddha tradition were saints only. Many were also tailors, poets, dancers, farmers, soldiers, even slaves, who realized God in the midst of their worldly life.

These worldly responsibilities are called our *dharma,* our duty. To pray to God so long and hard that we forget to feed our baby cannot be called prayer. Once a man came to Baba and said, "Baba, thanks to God's grace I haven't worked in twenty years." Baba said, "Show God some mercy and get a job!"

If you are a doctor, be a great doctor. If you're a mother, then you should be the best mother in the world. Of course, to pursue our duty like this is not always easy. Life throws all sorts of obstacles in our way. This is why Gurumayi often says we must behave like warriors. This doesn't mean we should be ferocious, but alert and brave. We should pursue our dharma with great enthusiasm and courage. A Roman philosopher said: "There is nothing so easy but that it becomes difficult through reluctance."

To live this way entails a certain amount of courage, an indifference to the pairs of opposites: heat and cold, pain and pleasure, praise and blame. But what else is new? A great being writes:

Having built one's house in the wilderness,
How can one afford to be afraid of the animals?

Having made one's house by the seashore,
How can one say he's afraid of the waves?

Having moved to the city,
Can one, in all seriousness,
Complain of the noise?

Hear what I say, O dear ones.
Having been born in this world,
One should not lose one's, temper
At praise or blame,
But maintain the poise of one's heart.[5]

This is yoga, the state of steady wisdom. Problems arise, problems dissolve. Don't dwell on them. Remember the Guru, have faith in God. God, who brought you this far safely, will surely not abandon you now.

RENUNCIATION

But what about renunciation? Surely all the scriptures of every path say that the world must be renounced. This is true. But what do these scriptures mean by renunciation?

Baba used to tease seekers who came to him expressing a desire to leave the world. "Leave the world?" he'd ask them, looking shocked. "And where do you intend to live? On the moon?"

The Siddhas force us to understand spiritual truths in a subtle and deeper way. Renunciation, they insist, does not mean abandoning one's duties, money, family life, or home. If being poor and idle made a man holy, then every derelict would be a saint.

True renunciation is an inner state, an attitude of nonattachment and surrender to the will of God. It is being *in* the world, but not *of* it. As long as we feel we are this body, and that this house, this family, this money, is "ours," we "give hostages to fortune" and will surely suffer.

KARMA YOGA

To avoid this suffering, the yogic scriptures urge us to perform all our worldly duties to the best of our ability but with an attitude of nonattachment. Do not confuse this detachment with not caring or with emotional coldness. In fact, only when we have this detachment can we perform our duties well. A surgeon, for instance, is forbidden to operate on members of his own family for precisely this reason. If he is emotionally embroiled in whether the patient will live or die, he will never be able to make the first incision. In the same way, yoga says, it is our passionate attachment to life which interferes with our living it as well and as happily as we are meant to.

When we give up this attachment while performing our duty, our life unfolds naturally and well.

SURRENDER TO GOD

There once lived a king who was oppressed and burdened by the demands of his kingdom. He longed to renounce his throne and live a simple life, serving God and his Guru. So he went to his Guru and told him of his desire.

The Guru thought for a moment, then said, "All right, O King. I will relieve you of your burden. Give your kingdom to me."

"Gladly," the king said. "It is yours."

The Guru thought for a moment. "The only problem,

King, is that I am a Guru. I teach meditation and the love of God, helping seekers make the inner journey. I have no time to administer a large kingdom. Therefore, O King, as your seva to me, rule my kingdom for me. Go back to your palace and take up your duties once again. But remember, O *Maharaj*, the kingdom is no longer yours."

The king returned to the palace and did as he had been instructed. He lived exactly as he had before, except now he found that his burden had been removed. Just as a rich man's accountant doesn't weep when his client loses money or rejoice when his client makes a fortune, since it is all the same to him, so the king ruled the kingdom with a calm mind and a peaceful heart.

Baba writes of such a king:

Once he had received the grace of the Guru and the knowledge that the universe is pervaded by God, the King saw that his throne, his subjects, his wife, and his relatives were all filled with the play of Consciousness, and that they were aids to happiness and full of happiness. Now he found the highest joy in the things that had once driven him wild with pain. He accepted the position given him by his destiny and passed his days ruling his kingdom. He saw Jagadish, the Lord of the Universe, in the heat of the sun, in mountain peaks, in the courses of flowing rivers, in the jumping waves of the ocean, in the deluges of the rainy season, in the lightning of the clouds, in the fields of yellow, green, and blue, and in the immense spaces of the skies. He experienced the pulsations of Chiti, Consciousness, in hunger and thirst, hope and despair, nearness and distance, justice and injustice, greed and contentment, anger and agitation. In spite of seeing differences in the outside world, inwardly he experienced non-differentiation. He had fully realized the Truth. He saw the light of his inner Self in his carriages, his jewelry, his food

*and drink, in God, man, seer and sage, in wood and in
stone. He would find God in all names, forms, qualities
and principles of the moving and unmoving universe.*[6]

NATURAL SAMADHI

This is the final stage of the spiritual journey. In it, the
hero, having defeated the dragon and reclaimed the
maiden, returns home with his prize. The dragon, of
course, is our limited identity with its animal appetites
and brute understanding, while the maiden we must re-
cover and marry is our true inner Self. Having become
who we always were, having found what was never lost,
we return to the world and take up the reins of our life
once more. Only now everything is different.

On the Siddha path, this final state is known as *sajaha
samadhi,* the natural state. It is the state of a Siddha, a
liberated being. "Such a one," Baba writes, "does not
have to retire to a cave or a desolate forest. He does not
have to force his eyes to remain closed or suspend his
breath to pass into inert samadhi. He is always in natural
samadhi, while eating, drinking, sleeping, waking, playing, talking, bathing, enjoying sense-pleasures, and meditating. He always lives in spontaneous joy."[7]

This is the greatness of the supreme adventure. When
the adventure is over, the hero returns with his prize to
the upper world. And yet here, too, there is a mystery. To
find your Self, you must lose yourself. To possess the
world, we must open our hands and possess nothing, giving up our pride of class and body, and our attachment to
this life. Gurumayi concludes:

*And as you free yourself from everything and every-
body, every place and every time, every moment and
every year, every planet and every star, you feel this*

incredible rush of ecstasy. And, in fact, you enter into another realm, an expanded realm, a realm of light, a realm of understanding. And it is inside. Even though we feel it is an out-of-the-body experience, it is within this body. And when you have this experience, you become aware of how this body is not a barrier, not an obstacle. In this body, there is honey. In this body, there are gold coins. In this body, there is a ruby. Kabir describes his Beloved as a ruby, so brilliant, so beautiful. This ruby represents the Self within. This is why it is said, the wealth is inside. By detaching ourselves from everything and everyone, we get in touch with our own Self, and the Self within everybody and everything. And this is called love. It is for this you meditate. It is for this you live—to taste this beautiful life inside. It's an adventure to go deeper and deeper within, higher and higher within, and constantly come across incredible wealth, unknown things. Sometimes it is great love, and sometimes it is great ecstasy. Sometimes it is deep sorrow, sometimes it is unbearable grief. Whatever it is, it is the play of Consciousness. Becoming aware of this incredible play within, you become totally free from everything and everyone. Then wherever you carry your body, you do it because it is a joy. Where you take your mind, you do it because it's such an accomplishment. Then life is no longer a burden, nor are you a burden on this earth. Your existence is the delight of this earth, and this earth is a delight for you. It is for this ecstasy, this constant ecstasy, constant love, that we go inside— deeper and deeper, higher and higher. As we detach ourselves from all this, we get in touch with the heart of every cell, every particle of dust, this entire universe. And as we experience this oneness, this unity, our heart throbs, and pulsates with such love, with such longing. This is the ultimate experience.[8]

Afterword

Late one cool September night, as Gurumayi was preparing to leave the ashram in South Fallsburg for India, I found myself in an outdoor courtyard, sitting at her feet. Before us was a roaring fire, whose flames made the courtyard dance and glitter as though alive. Into these flames Gurumayi was pouring oil and *ghee,* sugar, honey, and herbs, as though feeding a voracious child. Finally, when the fire had been heated and sweetened, several enormous mailbags filled with thousands of letters from seekers and devotees were fed into the flames—letters she had read and answered over the course of her two-month stay.

And as the letters burned, limning themselves in black and gold, she threw back her head and murmured in ecstasy, "So much love!"

Later that night she referred to the fire as the *mahapuja* —the Great Worship—and at that moment I glimpsed the world through her eyes. What to me was just a bonfire, like the kind I'd roasted marshmallows around at camp, to her was a holy sacrifice, a divine presence, the worship of God. Through the power of her realization, the bricks and grass and mortar of the Catskill night had been transmuted into Consciousness, the world had come alive, and even the smoke of a midnight bonfire in which letters were burning, twisting, and curling was imbued with so much sweetness and love.

A few days later, Patti and I moved from our apartment in Manhattan to a place in the country. When all the boxes were packed, we brought them out to the elevator. Then I went back for one final look. As I stepped into the apartment, however, the door slammed shut behind me. I would have said it had been blown shut by the wind had I not made a point of locking all the windows. I tried to open the door, but it wouldn't budge. It was stuck. I twisted and turned the locks, but it still wouldn't open. Bending down and putting my eye to the crack, I saw the problem: a screw had worked its way out of the jamb and was blocking the door from opening.

For a while I tried to jimmy it, but it still wouldn't budge. Beginning to panic, I started to pound on it, while Patti now began to pound on the other side. The elevator had arrived, and now, when I still couldn't get out, she told me she was going to get a security guard to try to help us force it open. Suddenly I remembered the mantra. I said *Om Namah Shivaya,* tried the door again, and it opened at once.

Just then the security guard arrived. He was laughing, delightedly. He looked at me and said, "Your apartment loves you so much, it doesn't want you to go." Then he said it again. "Your apartment loves you so much, it doesn't want you to go." Finally, as though I hadn't heard him, he said a third time, "Your apartment loves you so much, it doesn't want you to go!" And as he said it the third time I knew that he was speaking the truth.

We had left the apartment without so much as a farewell. And yet we had done so much sadhana there, so much chanting, so much meditation that the brick and plaster had been transfigured; it had become alive, imbued with Consciousness. And I realized then that, like the fire I had seen in Gurumayi's court, the apartment was a conscious entity, a holy place, and not to be insulted or ignored.

So I went back inside and asked its forgiveness for leaving it so unceremoniously. I thanked it for keeping the rain off our heads, for giving us a place to study the scriptures and worship the Self, for all the visions I had seen in it and all the joy I had felt, and for providing a space where I could write without the wind blowing away the pages. I did not say this to the plaster walls or to the wooden studs, but to that living Consciousness which exists in everything and is at the root of all things. Then, with a respectful bow, I locked the door and left.

As we drove north that evening through the autumn twilight, the landscape seemed to pulse and shimmer with a subtle radiance, a supernatural light. For a moment, as I gazed at it, my blindness was dissolved and I saw that there was really only Consciousness playing everywhere in different forms. It was as though the gates of some enchanted castle, under a spell of sleep for ages, had opened again, and everything come to life.

Notes

Those quotes of Baba's and Gurumayi's which are without footnotes are taken from their talks, and were either transcribed by the author or by others. With scriptural quotations, I have tried to always give a source, if not a chapter and a verse; those whose sources are not cited were quoted nonetheless by either Swami Muktananda or Gurumayi Chidvilasananda.

THE SIDDHA PATH: AN INTRODUCTION

1. "Nana margaistu dushprayam/ kaivalyan paramam padam/ siddhi margena labhate/ nanyatha padma sambhava." (*Yogashikha Upanishad*, I.1–3).

PART I: THE VISION OF YOGA

1. Robert Bly, *Kabir. Try to Live to See This!* (Denver: The Ally Press, 1976), p. 1.

2. *Chandogya Upanishad*, VIII.1.6 and VIII.5.3 (Swami Prabhavananda and Frederick Manchester, trans., *The Upanishads. Breath of the Eternal* [Hollywood, CA: Vedanta Press, 1978]), pp. 74 and 76.

3. Kabir, translated by the author. Also see Rabindranath Tagore, trans., *Songs of Kabir* (New York: Samuel Weiser, Inc., 1977).

4. Swami Muktananda, *Mukteshwari* (Oakland: SYDA Foundation, 1980), p. 16.

5. Swami Muktananda, *Secret of the Siddhas* (South Fallsburg, NY: SYDA Foundation, 1980), p. 2.

6. For more information on the historical sources of yoga, the reader may wish to consult Alain Danielou's fascinating *Shiva and Dionysus* and Mircea Eliade's *Yoga: Immortality and Freedom,* as well as Joseph Campbell's *The Mythic Image* and *Masks of God: Oriental Mythology.*

7. "Vismayo yogabhumikah." (Jaidev Singh, ed., *Siva Sutras. The Yoga of Supreme Identity* [Delhi: Motilal Banarsidass, 1979], I.12.)

Chapter 1. THE SELF

1. *Chandogya Upanishad,* VIII.3.2, trans. by the author.

2. "Chaitanyamatma" and "Tritayabhokta viresha." (Singh, *Siva Sutras,* I.1 and I.11).

Chapter 2. THE MIND

1. Swami Venkateshananda, trans., *Yoga Vasishtha* (Albany: State University of New York Press, 1984). See especially the beginning of The Second Discourse.

2. Bhartrihari, *Vairagya-Satakam,* verses 70–71, trans. by the author. For an additional reference see Swami Madhavananda's translation (Calcutta: Advaita Ashrama, 1976).

3. "Yogash chitta-vritti nirodhaha." (I. K. Taimni, trans., *The Science of Yoga* [*Yoga Sutras* of Patanjali] [Wheaton, IL: The Theosophical Publishing House, 1975], I.2).

4. One is reminded here of both the Gospel of John ("In the beginning was the Word") and the Hebrew Kabbalah, in which the universe is said to have been created from the alphabet.

5. The yogic scriptures make no distinction between thoughts and emotions. They say that both our thoughts

and our emotions are based on the power of these inner words.

6. Singh, *Siva Sutras,* I.2.

7. Swami Muktananda, *Siddha Meditation* (Oakland: SYDA Foundation, 1975), p. 46.

8. Jaideva Singh, trans., *Vijnana Bhairava, or Divine Consciousness* (Delhi: Motilal Banarsidass, 1979), p. 63.

Chapter 3. THE WORLD

1. Jaideva Singh, trans., *Pratyabhijnadrdayam. The Secret of Self-recognition* (3rd ed.; Delhi: Motilal Banarsidass, 1980), Sutras 5 and 9.

2. "Nartakatma." (Singh, *Siva Sutras,* III.9).

3. "Rango'ntaratma." (*Ibid.* III.10).

4. Jnaneshwar Maharaj, *Changadev Pasathi* (Letter to Changadev), trans. by the author.

5. *Ibid.*

6. *Ibid.*

7. Jnaneshwar Maharaj, *Amritanubhava* (The Nectar of Self-Awareness), trans. by the author.

Chapter 4. THE GURU

1. Bernard Malamud, *The Assistant* (New York: Dell Publishing Co., Inc., 1971), p. 116.

2. Lest anyone believe that this Guru–disciple relationship is tangential to yoga, they need only consult the Upanishads, the sacred books in which the "philosophy" of yoga first appears in written form. In one of the very earliest Upanishads, the *Brihadaranyaka,* written down around 700 B.C., a brahmin priest seeking spiritual instruction appeals to the king of Benares: "Please, sir, accept me as your disciple and teach me of the Absolute." The king, pleased by his request, agrees to teach the priest, telling him, "As a web comes out of a spider, or as sparks fly up from fire, so do all powers of life, all worlds, all gods, all beings arise from the Self."

It is revealing that this—our earliest glimpse of yoga in

literature—is in the form of a dialogue between a Guru and his disciple—for this is what the king and brahmin are. Nor is this merely an accident of history; the very word *upanishad* means "sitting close devotedly," conjuring up this association. The oldest graphic depiction of yoga, on a Mohenjo-daro seal, illustrates this definition: two devotees with folded hands are kneeling before a Guru who is seated on a dais in the full lotus.

It is interesting, too, that the Upanishad does not treat yoga as a religion. If it were, a priest, presumably, would know its secrets; yet as the Upanishad makes plain, the wisdom of yoga is not known to priests, but flows from the mysterious and kingly figure of the Guru.

Clearly, the Guru and yoga are intimately connected and have been from the beginning.

3. Nicephorus the Solitary (d. ca. 1340; of Mt. Athos, teacher of St. Gregory Palamas), in E. Kadloubovsky and G.E.H. Palmer, eds., *Writings from the Philokalia on Prayer of the Heart* (London: Faber & Faber, 1951), p. 32.

4. "Sri Guru Gita," *The Nectar of Chanting* (So. Fallsburg: SYDA Foundation, 1983), verse 23.

5. *Ibid.,* verse 62.

6. Taimni, *Yoga Sutras,* I.26.

7. Singh, *Siva Sutras,* II.6.

8. "Gururva parameshwari anugrahika shaktihi." (*Ibid.,* commentary on Sutra 6 by Kshemaraja [*Siva Sutra Vimarshini*]).

9. "Sri Guru Gita," verse 110.

10. Singh, *Siva Sutras,* III.27–28.

11. *Ibid.,* commentary on Sutra 28 by Kshemaraja, p. 192.

Chapter 5. THE POWER

1. Swami Muktananda, *Light on the Path* (So. Fallsburg: SYDA Foundation, 1981), p. 14.

2. Singh, *Pratyabhijnahrdayam,* commentary on Sutra 1, p. 48.

3. "That *spanda shakti* is not different from Shiva, because Shiva is not different from Shakti. Both Shiva and Shakti refer to the same Reality, just as fire and heat are not two different things." Swami Muktananda translates this passage from the "Spanda scriptures" in his *Secret of the Siddhas* (So. Fallsburg: SYDA Foundation, 1980), p. 156.

4. *Kundalini Stavaha* (So. Fallsburg: SYDA Foundation, 1981), verse 1.

5. Swami Muktananda, *Kundalini, Secret of Life* (So. Fallsburg: SYDA Foundation, 1979), p. 39.

6. "Sri Guru Gita," verse 33.

7. *Svetashvatara Upanishad,* verse 115.

PART II: THE PRACTICES OF JOY

Chapter 6. MANTRA AND CHANTING: THE VEHICLE

1. *Mandukya Upanishad,* verse 1, trans. by the author.

2. Singh, *Siva Sutras,* II.6–7.

3. Joseph Chilton Pearce, *The Bond of Power* (New York: E. P. Dutton, 1981), pp. 140–1. The information on Alfred Tomatis comes from Mr. Pearce in conversation with the author.

4. Taimni, *Yoga Sutras,* II.44.

5. Swami Muktananda, *Understanding Siddha Yoga,* Vol. I (So. Fallsburg: SYDA Foundation, 1978), p. 100.

Chapter 7. MEDITATION: THE INNER JOURNEY

1. *Svetashvatara Upanishad,* II.13 (Prabhavananda, *The Upanishads*), p. 121.

2. *The Mahayoga Vijnana* (See *Play of Consciousness* for a fuller description of this turning point in Baba Muktananda's sadhana).

3. Swami Muktananda, *Play of Consciousness,* p. 107.

4. Swami Chidvilasananda, *Kindle My Heart:* a forth-coming book of talks by Gurumayi.

5. *Svetashvatara Upanishad,* II.11.

6. Consider this account by the nineteenth-century Ger-man Christian mystic Heinrich Suso, writing of himself in the third person: "One day whilst the Servitor was still at rest, he heard within himself a gracious melody by which his heart was greatly moved. And at the moment of the rising of the morning star, a deep sweet voice sang within him these words: *Stella maria maris, hodie processit ad ortum.* That is to say, Mary Star of the Sea is risen today. And this song which he heard was so spiritual and so sweet that his soul was transported by it and he too be-gan to sing joyously. . . ." (Evelyn Underhill, *Mysticism* [New York: New American Library, 1974]), p. 277.

7. Edith Hamilton, *Mythology* (New York: New Ameri-can Library, 1969 [1940]), p. 13. Hamilton also says, "Tri-ton was the trumpeter of the Sea. His trumpet was a great shell. He was the son of Poseidon and Amphitrite." (p. 38).

8. Swami Muktananda, *Kundalini, Secret of Life,* p. 39.

Chapter 8. STUDY AND SERVICE: LIGHT ON THE PATH

1. *Chandogya Upanishad,* IV.15.1 (Prabhavananda, *The Upanishads*), p. 68.

2. Swami Chidvilasananda, *Kindle My Heart.*

3. Swami Muktananda, *In the Company of a Siddha* (So. Fallsburg: SYDA Foundation, 1985), p. 142.

4. Swami Muktananda, *Play of Consciousness,* p. 147.

5. Swami Chidvilasananda, *Kindle My Heart.*

6. T. S. Eliot, *Four Quartets* (San Diego: Harcourt Brace Jovanovich, 1971), p. 59.

Chapter 9. SATSANG: THE COMPANY OF THE TRUTH

1. Hanumanprasad Poddar, trans., *Bhakti Sutras* [of Narada](Orissa: Orissa Cement Ltd., n.d.), Sutras 38–40.

2. Poem by the author.

3. Swami Muktananda, *I Have Become Alive. Secrets of the inner journey* (So. Fallsburg: SYDA Foundation, 1985), pp. 27–28.

Chapter 10. SIDDHA YOGA IN THE WORLD: VICTORY AND RETURN

1. "Yatha cha bhagawan vishvasharira"—The universe is God's body. (As quoted by Swami Muktananda in *Siddha Meditation*, p. 82.)

2. Abhinavagupta wrote several related treatises on aesthetics, including the *Abhinava Bharati, Kautuka Vivarana,* and parts of *Tantraloka.*

3. James Joyce, *A Portrait of the Artist as a Young Man* (21st edn; New York: Compass Books, Viking Press, 1956 [1916]), p. 205.

4. Taimni, *Yoga Sutras,* I.2 and I.37.

5. Unidentified poem quoted by Gurumayi Chidvilasananda in Manhattan, N.Y., on May 13, 1986.

6. Swami Muktananda, *Play of Consciousness,* p. 232.

7. Swami Muktananda, *Siddha Meditation,* p. 45.

8. Swami Chidvilasananda, *Kindle My Heart.*

Selected Bibliography

Those readers interested in further reading or study may wish to consult the following reference works and scriptures.

In the case of scriptures, I have listed those translations and commentaries which I believe are the most authentic and readable.

Swami Muktananda. *Play of Consciousness*. San Francisco: Harper & Row, 1978.

Transformation Volume Three: On Tour with Gurumayi Chidvilasananda. So. Fallsburg: SYDA Foundation, 1988.

SCRIPTURES

Bhagavad Gita. Translated by Swami Nikhilananda. New York: Ramakrishna-Vivekananda Center, 1978.

Bhakti Sutras: The Philosophy of Divine Love. Translated by Hanumanprasad Poddar. Orissa: Orissa Cement Ltd., n.d.

"Sri Guru Gita." *The Nectar of Chanting*. So. Fallsburg: SYDA Foundation, 1983.

Mahanirvana Tantra: The Tantra of the Great Liberation. Translated by Arthur Avalon (Sir John Woodroffe). New York: Dover Publications, 1972.

Siva Sutras: The Yoga of Supreme Identity. Translated by Jaideva Singh. Delhi: Motilal Banarsidass, 1979.

The Upanishads. Breath of the Eternal. Translated by Swami Prabhavananda and Frederick Manchester. Hollywood, CA: Vedanta Press, 1978.

Vairagya-Satakam, or The Hundred Verses on Renunciation [by Bhartrihari]. Translated by Swami Madhavananda. Calcutta: Advaita Ashram, 1976.

Vijnanabhairava or Divine Consciousness. Translated by Jaideva Singh. Delhi: Motilal Banarsidass, 1979.

Yoga Sutras of Patanjali. See *The Science of Yoga.* Translated by I.K. Taimni. Wheaton, IL: The Theosophical Publishing House, 1975.

Yoga Vasishtha. Translated by Swami Venkateshananda. Albany: State University of New York Press, 1984.

For more information about Siddha Yoga, write or call: SYDA Foundation, P.O. Box 600, South Fallsburg, N.Y. 12779, (914) 434-2000.

Glossary

ABHINAVAGUPTA (993–1015): commentator and exponent of Kashmir Shaivism; of the lineage of Vasugupta and Somananda.

ANAHATA NADA: the inner divine melody; the "unstruck" sound heard in meditation. See also Nada.

ANANDA: absolute bliss.

ANAVA MALA: in Kashmir Shaivism, one of the impurities or limitations which brings about bondage of the universal Self and reduces it to a limited, individual being; the individual's innate ignorance of his true nature.

ASANA: (1) any one of various bodily postures practiced to strengthen the body, purify the nerves, and develop one-pointedness of mind; (2) a seat or mat on which one sits for meditation.

ASTRA: a sound-weapon described in the Mahabharata.

BAAL SHEM TOV: (1700–1760) Ukrainian teacher and religious leader who founded the Hasidic movement of Judaism.

BENARES (or Varanasi, Kashi): a holy city sacred to Shiva located in North India on the banks of the Ganges River.

BHAGAVAD GITA: the most popular of Hindu scriptures; a portion of the *Mahabharata* in which Lord Krishna instructs Arjuna about the path of liberation.

BHAKTI: divine love, devotion.

BHAKTI YOGA: the path of devotion leading to union with God; the state of intense devotional love for God or Guru.

BHARTRIHARI (5th century A.D.): a king who renounced his kingdom in order to become a yogi; author of many spiritual poems.

BHUKTI: worldly delights or pleasures.

BLUE PEARL: a tiny, shimmering light seen in meditation, and occasionally with open eyes, by people whose inner meditative energy has been awakened. The scriptures and saints call it the light of the inner Self.

BRAHMAN: Vedantic term for the Absolute Reality, or God.

CHAITANYA: live, conscious.

CHAKRA: literally, "wheel." In the human body there are seven major energy centers or nerve plexes called chakras.

CHIDVILAS: literally, "the play of Consciousness."

CHIN MUDRA: hand gesture in which the top of the thumb and index finger touch while the other three fingers are outstretched, practiced during meditation to keep the spiritual energy from flowing out of the body.

CHIT or CHITI: divine conscious energy; the creative aspect of God, portrayed as the universal Mother.

CHITSHAKTI: (1) the power of self-revelation by which the Supreme shines by itself; (2) universal Consciousness.

CONSCIOUSNESS: the intelligent, supremely autonomous energy that manifests, pervades, and supports everything in the cosmos.

DARSHANA: literally, "a seeing." In the East, any one of six schools of Indian philosophy.

DEVAYANA PANTHA: the way of the gods.

DHARANA: centering technique. See also *Vijnana Bhairava.*

DHARMA: duty; the law of righteousness.

FANA: literally, "passing away." The Sufi equivalent of enlightenment, or nirvana.

GANGES: the most sacred river in India, which flows from the Himalayas through North India.

GHEE: clarified butter.

GILGAMESH: a legendary Sumerian king who was the hero of Sumerian and Babylonian epics.

GREAT BEING: See Mahapurusha.

GURU: a spiritual Master who has attained oneness with God and who initiates others into the spiritual path and guides them to liberation.

GURU GITA: literally, "song of the Guru." A scripture in the form of a dialogue between Shiva and Parvati, which explains the identity of the Guru with the Absolute and describes the nature of the Guru, the Guru/disciple relationship, and meditation on the Guru.

GURUSEVA: See Seva.

HATHA YOGA: one of the eight classical yogas, by which the samadhi state is attained by uniting the ingoing and outgoing breath. Various bodily and mental exercises are practiced for the purpose of bringing about the even flow of the breath, thus stilling the mind.

JADA: inert; dead.

JAPA: the repetition of a mantra, usually in silence.

JNANA YOGA: the path of knowledge; the yoga of attaining supreme wisdom through intellectual inquiry.

JNANESHWAR (1275–1296): a highly revered poet-saint of Maharashtra whose commentary on the *Bhagavad-Gita*—*Jnaneshwari*—is regarded as one of the world's most important spiritual works.

KABIR (1440–1518): a renowned Indian poet-saint who was a weaver in Benares. His followers were both Hindu and Muslim, and his influence was a powerful one in overcoming religious factionalism.

KARMA: physical, mental, or verbal action; the results of such action.

KASHMIR SHAIVISM: a nondual philosophy that recognizes the entire universe as a manifestation of Chiti, or divine conscious energy.

KAURAVAS: one of the two warring armies in the epic *Mahabharata.*

KIRTAN: a devotional chant consisting of the names of God.

KOAN: a question or statement contemplated in Zen Buddhism for the purpose of achieving a moment of revelation or enlightenment.

KRIYA: a gross (physical) or subtle (mental, emotional) purificatory movement of the awakened kundalini Shakti. Kriyas purify the body and nervous system to allow a seeker to sustain the energy of higher states of conscious-ness.

KULARNAVA TANTRA: treatise on yoga; a basic work of the Kaula school of North Indian tantrism.

KUNDALINI: literally, "coiled one." The primordial Shakti, or cosmic energy, that lies coiled in the mu-ladhara chakra of every individual. When awakened, kundalini begins to move upward within the sushumna, the subtle central channel, piercing the chakras and initi-ating various yogic processes which bring about total pu-rification and rejuvenation of the entire being. When kundalini merges in the sahasrara, the spiritual center in the crown of the head, the individual self merges in the universal Self and one attains the state of Self-realiza-tion.

KUNDALINI YOGA: one of the eight classical yogas, whereby the aspirant awakens the kundalini Shakti and directs it upward through the chakras of the subtle body.

LAKSHMAN: brother of Lord Rama.

LAKSHMI: the goddess of wealth and prosperity and the consort of Vishnu.

LAYA YOGA: the yoga by which samadhi is attained through the absorption of the mind in inner lights or inner sounds.

LILA: divine play. Creation is often explained in the yo-gic scriptures as the lila, or play, of God.

MAHA: great.

MAHABHARATA: an epic composed by the sage Vyasa delineating the struggles of two families over a kingdom. The rich and varied story of the epic contains the defini-tive teaching on right action (dharma).

MAHAPURUSHA: literally, "great person." A saint or holy being.

MAHARAJ: king.

MAHAYOGA: literally, "the great yoga," because it contains the eight classical yogas. Another name for Siddha Yoga.

MAHIMNA: hymn.

MANTRA: a sacred word invested with the power to transform and protect one who repeats it.

MANTRA MALA: related mantras sung in sequence.

MANTRA-VIRYA: the perfect "I"-consciousness, which is the fountainhead of all the powers of potencies behind the mantra; Shiva-consciousness.

MATRIKA: letter or sound syllable which is the basis of all words and hence of all knowledge.

MAYA: the force that shows the unreal as real and presents that which is temporary and short-lived as permanent and everlasting; the power of illusion.

MOHINI: a form taken by Vishnu.

MUDRA: literally, "to give joy." Hatha yoga postures of the hands and arms.

MULADHARA CHAKRA: spiritual center at the base of the spine where the kundalini lies dormant.

NADA: the unstruck sound experienced in meditation.

NADI: a subtle channel within the body through which prana flows.

NARADA: a divine rishi, or seer, who was a great devotee and servant of God. He appears in the Puranas and is the author of the *Narada Bhakti Sutras,* the authoritative text on bhakti yoga.

NYASA: an esoteric spiritual technique in which prana is infused into the chakras and subtle body.

OM: the primal sound; sound or vibration from which the entire universe emanates. It is the inner essence of all mantras.

OM NAMAH SHIVAYA: a mantra meaning "Salutations to Shiva." Shiva denotes the inner Self. It is known as the great redeeming mantra because it has the power to grant worldly fulfillment as well as spiritual realization.

PANDAVA: one of the two warring families in the *Mahabharata.*

PARAMAHANSA: literally, "supreme swan." An honorific title given to a Self-realized Master.

PATANJALI: a great sage and author of the *Yoga Sutras.*

PITRULOKA: the world of ancestors.

PRANA: vital force.

PRANAYAMA: breathing exercises that lead to the control of the prana.

PRASAD: (1) a blessed or divine gift; (2) food that has been blessed by being offered to God.

PRATYABHIJNAHRDAYAM: literally, "the heart of the doctrine of recognition." A text of twenty sutras on Kashmir Shaivism with commentaries by Kshemaraja.

PUJA: worship.

RAJA YOGA: the yoga of eight steps, or limbs, directed toward the purification and control of the mind, through which the Self is realized.

RASA: taste; juice; elixir.

RUDRAM: a powerful Vedic chant in honor of Rudra (Shiva).

SADGURU: a true Guru; divine Master. See also Guru.

SADHANA: the practice of spiritual discipline.

SAHASRARA: thousand-petaled spiritual center at the crown of the head where one experiences the highest states of consciousness.

SAJAHA SAMADHI: the spontaneous state of samadhi that remains continuous and unbroken throughout the waking, dream, and deep-sleep states.

SAMADHI: state of meditative union with the Absolute.

SAMSARA: the cycle of birth and death; worldly illusion.

SAMSKARA: an impression of a past thought or action embedded in the subconscious.

SANKALPA: thought or will.

SANKHYA: an important philosophical school founded by the sage Kapilamuni, which views the world as composed of two ultimate realities: spirit (purusha) and matter (prakriti).

SAPTAH: a long ongoing chant, lasting for up to seven days.

SATCHITANANDA: the nature of the Supreme Reality. Sat is truth or being, that which exists in all times, in all places, and in all things; chit is consciousness, that which illumines all places, times, and things; ananda is absolute bliss.

SATSANG: literally, "the company of the Truth." A meeting of devotees for the purpose of listening to scriptural readings, chanting, or sitting in the presence of a holy being; the company of saints and devotees.

SEVA: selfless service to the Guru.

SHAKTI (also known as Chiti, kundalini, kundalini Shakti): the divine cosmic power which projects, maintains, and dissolves the universe, and which, when awakened in a seeker, brings about a spiritual evolution.

SHAKTIPAT: the transmission of spiritual power (Shakti) from the Guru to the disciple; spiritual awakening by grace.

SHANKARACHARYA (788–820): one of the greatest of India's philosophers and sages, who expounded the philosophy of absolute nondualism (Advaita Vedanta). In addition to his writing and teaching, he established ashrams in the four corners of India.

SHANTARASA: literally, "taste of peace."

SHIVA: a name for the all-pervasive Supreme Reality; one of the Hindu trinity, representing God as the destroyer. In his personal form he is portrayed as a yogi wearing a tiger skin and holding a trident, with snakes coiled around his neck and arms.

SHIVA SUTRAS: a Sanskrit text which Shiva revealed to the sage Vasuguptacharya. It consists of seventy-seven sutras, which were found inscribed on a rock in Kashmir. It is the major scriptural authority for the philosophical school of Kashmir Shaivism.

SIDDHA: a perfected yogi; one who has attained the highest state and become one with the Absolute.

SUSHUMNA: the central and most important of all the 72,000 nadis, located in the center of the spinal column and extending from the base of the spine to the top of the head. The six chakras are situated in the sushumna, and it is through the sushumna channel that the kundalini rises. See also: Chakra, Kundalini, Nadi.

SUTRA: an aphorism, or pithy saying.

SWADHYAYA: the chanting aloud of scriptures or sacred texts.

SWAMI: monk.

TANDRA: a meditative state resembling but different from the deep-sleep state, often accompanied by spiritual visions, precognition, astral travel, and other such supranormal experiences.

UPANISHADS: the teachings of the ancient sages that form the knowledge or end-portion of the Vedas. The central teaching of the Upanishads is that the Self of a human being is the same as Brahman, the Absolute. The goal of life is the realization of that Truth.

VEDANTA: a philosophical school founded by Badarayana that contains the philosophical teachings of the Upanishads and investigates the nature and relationship of the Absolute, the world, and the Self.

VIJNANA BHAIRAVA: an important text of Kashmir Shaivism containing one hundred twelve dharanas (centering techniques) through which the Absolute is realized.

VILAS: literally, "play."

VISHNU: the supreme Lord; one of the Hindu trinity of gods representing God as the sustainer.

VYASA: a great sage of ancient times, compiler of the Vedas and Puranas, and author of the *Mahabharata*.

YOGA: literally, "union." The state of oneness with the Self, God; the practices leading to that state.

YOGANIDRA: the state of tandra, also known as yogic sleep.

YOGA SUTRAS: Patanjali's treatise on yoga; the authoritative text on raja yoga.

YOGI: one who practices yoga.

YUGA: age. The scriptures envision a recurring cycle of four ages, each lasting hundreds of thousands of years, ending with the current one, the Kali Yuga.